DIESEL SPOTTER'S GUIDE UPDATE

BY JERRY A. PI̶̶̶̶̶̶̶̶̶̶ ̶̶̶̶̶̶̶̶̶̶̶̶LOUIS A. MARRE

Editor: Mike Schafer. Art Director: Lawrence Luser. Copy Editor: Burr Angle. Layout Artist: David Campbell.

Cover photograph of SCL BQ23-7 by Ernest H. Robl.

KALMBACH BOOKS.

PREFACE

Since THE SECOND DIESEL SPOTTER'S GUIDE appeared in 1973, the motive power scene in the United States has undergone a slow evolution. No radically new models have been brought into general use, but repeated orders for the models then in existence have brought us to a condition where many of the older locomotives listed in the 1973 book are rare, or altogether extinct. At first, your authors considered a book which would concentrate on all models remaining in service, but upon investigation we discovered that there are so many scattered survivors, often only on the rosters of individual users and short lines, that this would have meant reproducing over 90 per cent of THE SECOND DIESEL SPOTTER'S GUIDE. Since THE SECOND DIESEL SPOT-TER'S GUIDE is to remain in print, serving as a sort of "historic diesel spotter's guide" and to provide basic information about trucks and other locomotive components, we decided to focus this book on the power that has come on the scene since EMD introduced the 645 engine in 1965. This results in some overlap with the 1973 book, but only to maintain continuity and update production totals. (NOTE: Production totals shown as "None+" mean "None yet"; i.e., the locomotive was still in the catalog at press time.) Perhaps when the SD40-2 and its companions have at last become a closed book and new models are on the catalog pages, the "historical" works can be revised into a single volume.

In preparing this book, we have acceded to a long-standing request by readers to include contemporary electric locomotives and recent lightweight train power cars. Because upgraded power from capital rebuild programs has become a major source of "new" locomotives, a section on that phenomenon is included, as well as on another burgeoning subject, slugs.

Cutoff date: Models announced after May 1979 are not included.

Organization of this book: In a change from earlier SPOTTER'S GUIDES, this work is organized by functional type of locomotive rather than by builder.

The types are designated in the Table of Contents and a description of the factors relating to the functional definition precedes each chapter.

Corrections and additions: We welcome reader corrections and additions, to be sent to the authors via the publisher, for incorporation into future editions.

We thank readers of THE SECOND DIESEL SPOTTER'S GUIDE for their corrections.

Acknowledgments: No work on diesel locomotive production and identification can be assembled today without frequent reference to Don Dover's locomotive news magazine *EXTRA 2200 SOUTH*, since it exceeds all official sources for completeness and accuracy on locomotive statistics. This heavy debt is gratefully acknowledged, and we suggest that readers obtain a subscription to *EXTRA 2200 SOUTH*, P.O. Box 41417, Cincinnati, Ohio 45241. It is the logical companion to the DIESEL SPOTTER'S GUIDES, serving to expand the horizons that newcomers to the field may find opening for them in locomotive technology, and keep the veterans up to date. Deane Ellsworth of Amtrak, and the Electro-Motive and General Electric organizations were also very helpful. The several photographers who responded to the call for specialized illustration are indispensable, and their credit lines indicate our debt. To all, our sincere thanks.

JERRY A. PINKEPANK
St. Paul, Minn.

LOUIS A. MARRE
University of Dayton
Dayton, Ohio
February 11, 1979

SWITCHERS

The category "switchers" formerly gave little trouble to students of locomotive taxonomy. In the 1950's, it could safely be said that switchers were locomotives of 1200 h.p. or less, having the cab at one end of the hood. The few locomotives which had the cab at one end but had road-engine horsepower—such as the 2000 h.p. Fairbanks-Morse H20-44—could thus be easily treated as road engines despite their cab configuration. However, now we have 1500 and 2000 h.p. locomotives which are primarily intended for use in yards, although they may be equipped to operate occasionally on the road, and the distinction has blurred. Therefore, we have arbitrarily defined as switchers any locomotive having a platform at each end and the cab at one end of the hood, with no short hood. Of course, locomotives clearly intended as switchers, such as the 1974 Line GE center-cabs and the Faur Quarter Horse, are also included in the category even though they depart from our switcher definition.

There are several reasons why the former switcher category is relatively barren in contemporary locomotive catalogs. First, the original production of the 1940's and 1950's is still largely intact and capable of carrying on for a long time in the low-mileage service where they are used (and where because of the low mileage it is hard to generate sufficient return on investment for one-for-one replacement). Second, downgraded GP7 and GP9 power is filling many yard roles which new switchers would otherwise perform (hence the marketing of such locomotives as the MP15DC and MP15AC as dual road/yard engines of similar capacity to the GP7/GP9 power). Third, the builders do not price switchers attractively as compared to the light or medium road-switchers discussed in the two following chapters.

EMD SWITCHERS: 645E ENGINE, 1000, 1500 H.P. B-B

Model	A.c./d.c.	H.p.	Cyls.	Length	Truck centers	Period produced	Approx. No. of units sold		
							U.S.A.	Canada	Mexico
SW1000	D.c.	1000	8	44'-8"	22'-0"	6/66-10/72	118	None	None
SW1001	D.c.	1000	8	44'-8"	22'-0"	9/68-date	111 +[1]	2 +[1]	7 +[1]
SW1500	D.c.	1500	12	44'-8"	22'-0"	7/66-1/74	807	None	None
SW1504	D.c.	1500	12	46'-8"	23'-0"	5/73-8/73	None	None	60
MP15DC	D.c.	1500	12	47'-8"	24'-2"	2/74-date	205 +[1]	4 +[1]	3 +[1]
MP15AC	A.c.	1500	12	49'-2"	24'-8"	8/75-date	167 +[1]	0 +[1]	0 +[1]

[1] Production totals are through December 31, 1977.

When the 645E engine replaced the 567C and D engines in GM's catalog, the SW1000 and SW1500 emerged as the evolutionary successors to the 567C-engined 8- and 12-cylinder switchers, the SW900 and SW1200. The main external differences from the 567 engine switchers are the higher cab profile (resulting in a roofline curve of larger radius) and hood detail changes. These include a headlight/number indicator fairing reminiscent of the SW1200RS in Canada, the addition of a grid-protected air space around the ends of the radiator cores at the top front of the hood (the grid wraps around the hood top),

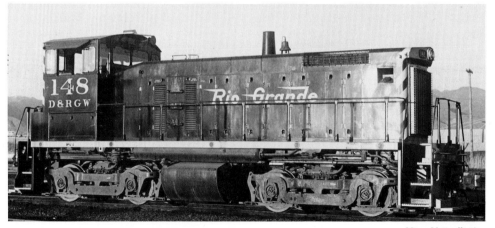

SW1000

This model is distinguished from the otherwise-similar SW1500 by having only a single stack instead of two, and by the short radiator opening at the top front of the hood, which does not extend over the sandbox fill as it does on the SW1500.

Marre-Mott collection.

and a new style of grid over the traditional EMD front radiator fan shutters.

The new cab profile caused clearance problems for industrial customers, and therefore EMD introduced the SW1001, with a lower cab and smaller-radius roofline curve. Only 21 SW1001's were produced through the end of 1972, when EMD apparently decided that the small market for the low-clearance 8-cylinder switcher did not warrant two designs in the catalog, and the SW1000 was dropped. Interestingly, there seems to have been no demand for a low-clearance 12-cylinder switcher even though several sales of high-clearance 12-cylinder switchers were made to industrial users. There appears to be nothing to prevent EMD from using a low cab on these SW1500 and MP15-series locomotives.

The SW1500 was the preferred switcher among railroad customers, but it faced a market limitation: More and more railroads wanted a locomotive that could perform as well in road service as in switching. The SW1500's short

frame prevented the use of the EMD Blomberg road truck and held down the weight of the locomotive. After in effect building a prototype in the form of 60 SW1504's for National Railways of Mexico in 1973, EMD solved the dual-service problem by introducing the lengthened MP15 in 1974. This allowed the B Flexicoil truck to be dropped from the catalog, except in the unlikely event of a customer ordering an SW1001 so equipped. The MP15 designation was changed to MP15DC when the MP15AC was introduced in 1975.

The MP15AC is, as its model designation implies, an MP15 fitted with an alternator/rectifier instead of the usual d.c. transmission, allowing a control system more compatible with larger EMD road locomotives. This model also has a road-engine-style radiator arrangement derived from the SD45T-2 and SD40T-2 models. Obviously aimed at the market niche occupied by aging GP7's and GP9's relegated to work in yards and on locals, the MP15AC's penetration was limited by the lack of a toilet, which some state laws require if

Continued

SW1500

SW1500

Both photos, Louis A. Marre.

Two stacks and a radiator opening at the top front of the hood which extends over the sandbox fill distinguish the SW1500 from the otherwise-similar SW1000. The Flexicoil trucks shown on K&IT 80 were optional; AAR type A were also used. In fact, K&IT 78 provides a droll illustration that, in a maintenance-related exchange on the owner railroad, the two trucks are interchangeable.

the unit is used outside of yards alone or in the lead of several units. The GP15-1 of 1976 did not have this drawback and appropriated much of what would otherwise have been the MP15AC market. The MP15AC continued to be ordered, though, in part because the GP15-1 was considerably more expensive unless the right type of trade-in (GP7, GP9, F7, F9, or other model with Blomberg B trucks) was provided. Thus, MP15AC's tended to be purchased by roads having non-EMD trade-ins or none at all. The cheaper MP15DC continued to be ordered by roads needing primarily a switcher, or by roads who did not feel the need for a.c. transmission.

Jack Armstrong.

SW1001

The hood on this model is identical to the SW1000, but the distinguishing feature is the low-profile cab.

SW1504

Virtually identical in appearance to the foot-longer MP15DC, the SW1504 is best distinguished by its being found only on NdeM, where there are (at this writing) no MP15DC's. However, the prominent louvered air filter box abaft the rear stack is a unique feature to the SW1504 as opposed to the MP15DC. The use of the Blomberg B truck instead of the Flexicoil B or AAR type A truck is the prime visual distinction from the SW1500.

MP15DC

The MP15DC is distinguished from the otherwise-similar SW1500 by the use of Blomberg B road trucks instead of the Flexicoil B or AAR type A trucks used on the latter. The air-filter box abaft the rear stack (not found on some MP15DC's) also distinguishes the model from the SW1500, and the lack of louvers in this box distinguishes the MP15DC from the SW1504. MP 1549 has the modified Blomberg truck with rubber instead of elliptical springs, and shock absorbers in the R1, R3, L2, and L4 positions.

Marre-Mott collection, James B. Holder.

MP15DC

Southern's variation on the MP15DC has an experimental muffler (which may soon appear on other locomotives to satisfy EPA standards) obscuring the dual stacks, and a bevel at the rear of the filter box. SOU 2348 also has conventional Blomberg B trucks instead of the modified version.

Marre-Mott collection, Warren Calloway.

MP15AC

The MP15AC is distinguished from the otherwise-similar MP15DC by the side-intake radiator arrangement, as shown in a detail photo made from MILW 492.

Both photos, Louis A. Marre.

MLW SWITCHERS: 251C ENGINE, 2000 H.P. B-B

Model	A.c./d.c.	H.p.	Cyls.	Length	Truck centers	Period produced	Approx. No. of units sold		
							U.S.A.	Canada	Mexico
M420TR	D.c.	2000	12	50'-0"	25'-4"	4/72	None	2	None
M420TR-2	D.c.	2000	12	57'-2"	32'-2"	7/75-date	None[1]	None[1]	15 +[1]

[1] Production totals are through December 31, 1977.

Using the same machinery as in the M420 road locomotives, the orders for this model to date—two M420TR's for Alcan, Ltd.'s Roberval & Saguenay, and 15 M420TR-2's for Mexico's Pacifico—may be regarded as custom-shop jobs, tailored to the needs of a particular customer. Presumably, most potential customers would find little price advantage in foregoing the flexibility of a conventional M420 to buy one of these machines.

Larry Russell collection, Dave More.

Only two units of this model were built, Roberval & Saguenay Nos. 26 and 27, unlikely to be confused with anything else.

M420TR

Both photos, Paul C. Hunnell.

M420TR Type 2

Only one order of this model had been built as of this writing, 15 units for Mexico's Ferrocarill del Pacifico. Since the cab end is considered front on the FCP units and has a distinctive eyebrow indicator/headlight/class light fairing, both ends are shown. The "1800 HP" under the number on the cab indicates derating by the railroad.

GE SWITCHERS: "1974 LINE", B-B CENTER-CAB

Model	A.c./d.c.	H.p.	Cyls.	Length	Truck centers	Period produced	Approx. No. of units sold		
							U.S.A.	Canada	Mexico
85-110 ton	D.c.	600	(2)6	44'-0"	22'-0"	8/74-date	9 +[1]	None +[1]	3 +[1]
125-144 ton	D.c.	1100	(2)6	48'-0"	25'-0"	12/75-date	3 +[1]	None	2 +[1]

[1] Production totals are through December 31, 1977.

Although the 1974 Line GE center-cabs are primarily intended as industrial locomotives, GE demonstrated the 144-ton model as a potential Class 1 railroad switcher. The first order by a Class 1 road was the lease by Chicago & North Western, for a period of two years starting in 1979, of Nos. 1198 and 1199, painted in full C&NW livery. Also, the 110-ton model was ordered by two industry-captive short lines, Wyandotte Southern and Moscow, Camden & St. Augustine. Distinguishing features of the 1974 Line locomotives are the slope-sided cab and the bead outlining the hood end.

Jerry A. Pinkepank.

Raymond F. Kucaba.

Wyandotte Southern's 110-tonner illustrates the 85-110 ton version of the 1974 Line locomotive. Note that the hood reaches practically to the stepwell, while on C&NW's 136-ton version of the 125-144 ton model the hood is one handrail stanchion spacing back of the stepwell, due to the longer frame.

FAUR SWITCHER: 1250 H.P. B-B

Model	A.c./d.c.	H.p.	Cyls.	Length	Truck centers	Period produced	Approx. No. of units sold		
							U.S.A.	Canada	Mexico
Quarter Horse	Hydr.	1250	6	43'-8"		1974	1	None	None

The Quarter Horse is a Romanian product marketed in the United States by Stanray Corp. It demonstrated on several Class 1 railroads but was never ordered. The demonstrator was sold in 1978 to the Washington (D.C.) Terminal Company.

The initials FAUR stand for Romanian words translating, approximately, "Consolidated Rolling Stock Factory," a nationalized enterprise, of course. The engine is said to be a Sulzer design built under license and the transmission is Voith. Due to Morrison-Knudsen promoting the Sulzer engine, and Voith transmissions having been used on a number of lightweight train power cars in the U.S., including recent Amtrak turbos, the Quarter Horse might not be quite the orphan it appears.

Marre-Mott collection, Gordon B. Mott.

LIGHT ROAD-SWITCHERS

The term "light road-switcher" is one we have used in the DIESEL SPOTTER'S GUIDES to identify road locomotives designed for local and branchline freight and passenger duties, created by placing switch-engine machinery on a lengthened frame with road trucks and a short hood. The short hood could house steam generator equipment if the unit were to be used in passenger service. The fact that space for a steam generator no longer needs to be provided for in such designs has blurred the distinction, since the short hood now shelters only the collision posts for cab-forward operation and is usually where the toilet is placed. An end-cab locomotive such as the MP15AC could be fitted with a toilet under the long hood and run long-hood forward in road service with little practical distinction from what we call a light road-switcher. However, the lengthened frame of the GP15-1, for example, allows room for the designer to provide the essentials of road locomotive equipment, and allows the locomotive to be heavier, which helps tractive effort.

EMD LIGHT ROAD-SWITCHER: 645E ENGINE, 1500 H.P. B-B

| Model | A.c./d.c. | H.p. | Cyls. | Length | Truck centers | Period produced | Approx. No. of units sold | | |
							U.S.A.	Canada	Mexico
GP15-1	D.c.	1500	12	54'-11"	29'-9"	6/76-date	110 + [1]	None + [1]	None + [1]

[1] Production totals are through December 31, 1977.

The GP15-1 represents a further slight evolution from the MP15AC in EMD's attempt to solicit orders based on GP7/GP9 trade-ins. The locomotive is designed to make the greatest possible use of components from these trade-ins, and when such trade-ins are furnished, the price is competitive with contractor or railroad shop rebuild jobs. The increase in length over the MP15AC provides for better weight distribution on bridges, better tracking at road speeds, and allows room for a toilet and a road-engine-style cab with collision-protection short hood.

Louis A. Marre.

Gordon B. Mott.

C&NW and SLSF ordered their GP15-1's without inertial air filters, hence the louvering by the cab for conventional filters at the top of the hood.

Both GP15-1

Missouri Pacific's version with inertial filters is represented by MP 1577.

Marre-Mott collection, Jack Armstrong.

GE LIGHT ROAD-SWITCHER: 7FDL8 ENGINE, 1800 H.P. B-B

Model	A.c./d.c.	H.p.	Cyls.	Length	Truck centers	Period produced	Approx. No. of units sold		
							U.S.A.	Canada	Mexico
U18B	D.c.	1800	8	54'-8"	30'-8"	3/73-10/76	118	None	45

Although we defined light road-switchers as locomotives having switch-engine machinery on road-engine frame and trucks, GE never built an 1800 h.p. switch engine (though they offered one). However, the U18B clearly belongs in the same market as the GP15-1, and probably helped bring the GP15-1 into existence when two railroads, SCL and MEC, traded old EMD power for U18B's. Interestingly, the end of U18B production practically corresponds with the start of GP15-1 production. At this writing, no equivalent B18-7 has appeared.

Marre-Mott collection, Tom King.

U18B

When trade-in trucks were not re-used, the U18B used the two-axle Floating Bolster truck seen on SCL 252. On the other hand, MEC 405 (opposite page) shows the use of EMD Blomberg B trucks from a trade-in.

Marre-Mott collection, J. R. Quinn.

U18B

Quick spotting feature for a U18B is to count the power assembly access doors, the tall doors where "405" appears on the hood side of this MEC unit. A U18B has four door panels, a U23 has six, and a U30B has eight, corresponding to the number of power assemblies on a side, to which access is provided.

MEDIUM ROAD-SWITCHERS, B-B

The medium- or intermediate-horsepower road-switcher came into existence in the late 1960's to fill a gap in the horsepower range of then available locomotives. Many applications called for a locomotive larger than a switcher, but did not justify the acquisition and maintenance costs of a 3000-3600 maximum-horsepower locomotive. This left room for motive power in the 2000-2300 h.p. range. Although early sales of the medium-horsepower units were modest, they soon demonstrated their economies for certain jobs and have become increasingly popular.

EMD MEDIUM ROAD-SWITCHERS: 645E ENGINE, 2000, 2300 H.P. B-B

Model	A.c./d.c.	H.p.	Cyls.	Length	Truck centers	Period produced	Approx. No. of units sold		
							U.S.A.	Canada	Mexico
GP38	D.c.	2000	16	59'-2"	34'-0"	1/66-12/71	466	21	6
GP38AC	A.c.	2000	16	59'-2"	34'-0"	1971	240	0	0
GP38-2	A.c.	2000	16	59'-2"	34'-0"	1/72-date	1269 + [1]	115 + [1]	95 + [1]
GP38P-2[2]	A.c.	2000	16	59'-2"	34'-0"	6/75	None[1]	None[1]	20[1]
GP39	A.c.	2300	12	59'-2"	34'-0"	5/69-7/70	21	0	0
GP39DC	D.c.	2300	12	59'-2"	34'-0"	6/70	2	0	0
GP39-2	A.c.	2300	12	59'-2"	34'-0"	8/74-date	135	0	0

[1] Production totals are through December 31, 1977.
[2] "GP38P-2" designation not official; these units were ordinary GP38-2's with a high nose and steam generator.

When the 645E engine replaced the 567C and D engines in GM's catalog, the GP38 was introduced as a 3-foot-longer version of the otherwise-similar 567-powered GP28. Although the GP28 had enjoyed very limited sales during the 20-month period in which it was produced, EMD perceived that there was a market for a less-than-3000 h.p. locomotive, especially one without a turbocharger (which is a maintenance headache if not needed for higher output). The GP38 was the result. However, EMD also felt that some customers would rather take the turbocharger and four fewer power assemblies, so it offered the GP39 as an alternative. As it turned out, only Chesapeake & Ohio, with 20 units (3900-3919), and Atlanta & St. Andrews Bay with one unit (507) opted for the turbocharger; Kennecott Copper ordered their units (Nos. 1 and 2) fitted with a d.c. generator instead of an alternator. Therefore, when the Dash 2 line appeared in January 1972, no mention was made of a GP39-2. Subsequently, however, customers requested the model, which EMD had previously indicated would be available on special order. The first customer was AT&SF, who wanted the turbocharger for operation at high altitudes, such as between Pueblo and Denver where the line is all above 5000 feet elevation (non-turbocharged locomotives lose considerable output at high altitudes because of the thin air, and may also smoke objectionably). The next customer was Reading, to whom the old argument of four fewer power assemblies must have appealed—Reading had no altitude problems. The GP39-2 went on to a respectable production figure. The GP38-2 was nonetheless a runaway favorite, because GP38's and GP38-2's already in service soon acquired an exceptional reputation for high availability and low operating cost. National Railways of Mexico ordered 20 of them equipped with high hoods housing steam generators for passenger service, and they carried an unofficial model number of "GP38P-2." Since there was no change in the locomotive except for the steam generator (high-hood versions were also furnished to N&W and SR to satisfy their penchants for a two-ended locomotive that crews would not object to

operating long-end forward), there really was no basis for a separate model number, except that 1975 was such a late date to be building a steam-equipped locomotive that the distinction seemed worthwhile. From a design standpoint the main difference between the GP38-2 and the GP38 was the use of modular electronics on the Dash 2. Also, a "high traction" version of the Blomberg truck was offered as an option on the Dash 2, but it was not as significant a departure from design as the HT-C truck on the SD40-2. One last model to be mentioned is the GP38AC, which was offered as an option to the regular DC model during 1971. There is no visible external difference between the AC and DC models.

Both GP38

Both photos, Louis A. Marre.

DT&I 216 illustrates a GP38 with paper air filters but with no dynamic braking. The two stacks in line (highlighted by spark arresters on DT&I 216) instead of the single, crosswise turbocharger stack distinguish the non-turbocharged GP38 from otherwise similar models. The 567-engined GP28 is very similar in appearance but three feet shorter; on a GP28 there is no space between the front edge of the radiator and the first of the power-assembly access doors from the rear (on which the letter "I" is stenciled on DT&I 216). Since only 26 GP28's were built, 10 of them for Mexico, the opportunity for confusion does not often arise. B&O 3845 is a GP38 with normal-range dynamic braking (extended range braking would be indicated by an access door for contactors in the blank portion of the blister). B&O 3845 lacks the paper air-filter feature, which would appear as a box raised a little above

the hood line and cut off the end of the dynamic brake blister fairing toward the cab (see the location of the box on DT&I 216). Here the twin stacks are barely visible in the form of triangular spark screens. The twin fans over the radiators, however, remain visible, as distinct from three such fans on a GP40, or two such fans spaced by a smaller fan on the 567-engined GP35.

Both GP38-2

No single spotting feature is totally reliable in distinguishing a GP38-2 from a GP38. MKT 311 is a GP38-2 with conventional Blomberg B trucks, paper air filter, and no dynamic braking. Only the lack of a hinged battery box cover with latches, and the stubbier radiator area with fans more closely spaced, shows the locomotive to be a Dash 2 in this case. However, the first few GP38-2's had the old radiator arrangement, and BN GP38-2's have the hinged battery box covers specially ordered by the railroad. TP&W 2001 is a later GP38-2 with the paper air filter box faired down. This was first done on special order for the LIRR order delivered starting in January 1976. EMD then made it a standard item on all subsequent GP38-2's equipped with paper air filters. The change in the radiator area is more evident by comparing TP&W 2001 with DT&I 216. The stacks of TP&W 2001 are not visible, but from this angle a turbocharger stack would be, so they can be inferred. The oblong water-level sight glass below and to the right of the radiator is a right-side-only detail on most Dash 2's.

Marre-Mott collection, James B. Holder.

Louis A. Marre.

Marre-Mott collection, James B. Holder.

Both GP38-2

L&N 4125 is a GP38-2 with the optional Blomberg High Traction truck (note the rubber spring and shock absorbers), paper air filters, and extended-range dynamic braking. CN 5595 is equipped with a so-called Comfort Cab. As of December 31, 1977, there were 51 GP38-2's on CN so equipped (starting in 1973) along with 60 built previously with conventional cabs. The CN units were the only Comfort Cab GP38-2's.

Marre-Mott collection, Larry Russell.

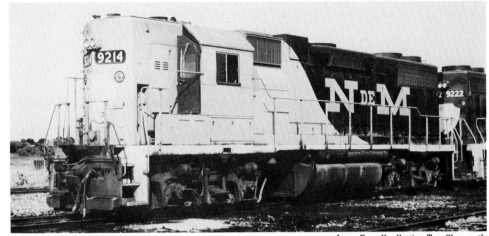

GP38P-2

The 20 steam generator-equipped GP38-2's built for NdeM in 1975 were unofficially tagged GP38P-2's, but except for the steam generator they are the same as high-hood GP38-2's built for N&W and Southern.

GP39

C&O 3916 illustrates the position of the single, fat turbocharger stack set crosswise on the roofline where the paper air-filter box is located on GP38's so equipped. The combination of this stack with just two fans indicates a GP39 or GP39-2. The distinctions for the Dash 2's are similar to those for the GP38, but since C&O 3900-3919, A&StAB 507, and Kennecott 1 and 2 are the only GP39's, the opportunity for confusion does not often arise.

GP39-2

D&H 7613 also exhibits the turbocharger stack, and is equipped with the high-traction truck option. Interestingly some GP39-2's such as D&H 7613 reverted to the old GP38 radiator (spanning all or part of six door panels), while later units had the GP38-2 version spanning just four door panels. Apparently the smaller radiator was at first thought not to be sufficient for the cooling demands of 300 more horsepower but later experience must have proved otherwise.

Marre-Mott collection, J. R. Quinn.

GP39-2

Kennecott Copper Company took delivery of 11 GP39-2's in January 1977 with a special-order cab configuration and a high under-clearance for rocks found on the track in its Bingham (Utah) open pit mine.

Paul C. Hunnell.

GE MEDIUM ROAD-SWITCHERS: FDL12 ENGINE, 2250 H.P. B-B

Model	A.c./d.c.	H.p.	Cyls.	Length	Truck centers	Period produced	Approx. No. of units sold		
							U.S.A.	Canada	Mexico
U23B	D.c.	2250	12	60'-2"	36'-2"	8/68-6/77	425	None	40
B23-7	A.c.	2250	12	62'-2"	36'-2"	9/77-date	169 + [1]	None + [1]	None + [1]
BQ23-7	A.c.	2250	12	62'-2"	36'-2"	11/78-date	10 + [1]	None + [1]	None + [1]

[1] Production totals are through December 31, 1978 (preliminary).

GE waited for a year after EMD had raised its 16-cylinder engine from 2500 to 3000 h.p. rated output (with the introduction of the 645 engine) before raising the FDL16 from 2800 to 3000 h.p. When this was done, the GE catalog was left without an intermediate-size locomotive. There was some question as to whether such a market existed, because up to that point railroads had been looking for higher horsepower to accomplish unit reduction when replacing 1500-1800 h.p. locomotives in mainline service. However, as the GP38 began to produce sales, GE decided to offer a 12-cylinder, 2250 h.p. locomotive to compete, using the U30B carbody. The result was the U23B, and respectable sales followed. With the introduction of the Dash 7 line, the B23-7 succeeded the U23B. The BQ23-7 is simply a standard B23-7 with a so-called "Quarters Cab" having extra space for a conductor's desk for operation on cabooseless trains. This cab is available on any GE Dash 7 locomotive. Because the 1978 National Agreement with the UTU failed to establish a policy for the caboose and crew consist issue that would be accepted by all carriers, the individual railroads were left to negotiate their own agreements, and the use of the Quarters Cab locomotives will probably follow the course of local agreements.

U23B

Louis A. Marre

Marre-Mott collection, Ken Douglas.

U23B

WP 2258 is a U23B on trade-in EMD Blomberg B trucks; AT&SF 6308 (facing page) is a U23B on the AAR type B trucks otherwise furnished (floating-bolster trucks were an option). Otherwise identical to contemporary U30B's, the U23B's can be identified by the number of power assembly access doors, the taller doors in mid-hood on which the letters TERN from "Western Pacific" appear on 2258, and the letters ANT on AT&SF 6308. There are six door panels on U23's versus eight door panels on U30's, reflecting the number of power assemblies on a side.

Both photos, Louis A. Marre.

L&N 5129 is a standard B23-7. The door panel means of identification (see previous page) continues in the B23-7's, though the overall carbody is two feet longer than the U23B. The power assembly access doors are just forward of the step in the hood which is an identifying feature of the Dash 7 line. The wide radiator is also a Dash 7 feature, as is the floating-bolster truck unless a trade-in truck is used.

This "step" in the hood, characteristic of all 7-series GE locomotives, is the result of the hood being widened to accommodate an angled, elevated position of the oil cooler, which allows it to drain and thereby reduces winter freeze damage when the locomotive is shut down. The former position of the oil cooler was vertical and at floor level.

B23-7

B23-7

BQ23-7

SOU 3971 is a standard B23-7 except for the high short hood; SCL 5131 illustrates the Quarters Cab (BQ23-7) option.

MLW MEDIUM ROAD-SWITCHERS: 251C ENGINE, 2000 H.P. B-B

Model	A.c./d.c.	H.p.	Cyls.	Length	Truck centers	Period produced	Approx. No. of units sold		
							U.S.A.	Canada	Mexico
M420	A.c.	2000	12	60'-10"	36'-5"	5/73-date	None[1]	92 + [1]	None[1]
M420B	A.c.	2000	12	60'-10"	36'-5"	6/75-7/75[1]	None[1]	8[1]	None[1]
M420R	A.c.	2000	12	60'-10"	36'-5"	2/74-5/75[1]	5[1]	None[1]	None[1]

[1] Production totals are through December 31, 1977.

During the period when MLW was building Alco designs under license, no equivalent of the Century 420 was sold in Canada. Instead, MLW continued the 1800 h.p. RS18 to June 1968 and also built 92 Century 424's through May 1967 for CN and CP. In 1969, MLW purchased Alco's engineering designs and took over Alco's worldwide locomotive licensing agreements. They replaced the Century line with their own "M" line of Montreal-designed power, which was still being built around the 251 engine and GE electrical equipment that had characterized the Alco-licensed production. During the 1969-72 period, MLW contented itself with M630's and M636's for domestic markets (except for the experimental M640) but dabbled for over two years from 1970 with a 2000 h.p.

design for the Roberval & Saguenay, finally delivered in 1972 as the M420TR. The M420 followed shortly, but as an a.c. machine with the so-called "Comfort Cab" which had just come into use in Canada that year. The M420B was simply a cabless version designed to be used as a radio-controlled mid-train helper for the British Columbia Railway, while the M420R was a version designed to use trade-in components from Alco RS3's (mainly trucks) for the Providence & Worcester. Since these latter two models have not been repeated in over three years, they are shown in the table as if production had ceased, although nothing would appear to prevent their being built in a future order.

M420

Marre-Mott collection, Larry Russell.

M420

CN 2505 and BCOL 645 (facing page) are M420's without and with dynamic braking. The openings in the upper part of the hood behind the cab show the difference; the CN unit has just the central engine air intake in this position, while the BCOL unit has the dynamic brake grid cooling openings behind the air intake. The middle square in the dynamic brake grouping is a bare, unprotected dynamic brake resistor grid. It is unusual that this is not protected by screening because of potential heat and shock hazard to personnel during dynamic braking. Notice that on BCOL M420B No. 688, built two years later than 645, the grids are covered and only the air vents are visible. The truck used on the M420 and M420B is the MLW high-adhesion truck known as the Zero Weight Transfer or ZWT truck.

M420B

In this view of BCOL 688 we are looking at what would be the cab end, as evidenced by the position of the central air intake, dynamic brake cooling openings, and, at the opposite end, the radiator. Radio control equipment is housed in "cab" end of the hood.

Marre-Mott collection, Larry Russell.

M420R

P&W 2004 is similar to the standard M420 except for use of trade-in Alco AAR type B trucks. All MLW 420's are most readily distinguished from other Comfort Cab locomotives by the bevel along the top edge of the hood.

Marre-Mott collection, Ken Douglas.

HIGH HORSEPOWER ROAD-SWITCHERS, B-B

From 1959 through 1965, the B-B locomotive was the focus of heavy competition among EMD, Alco, and GE to see who could cram the most horses into a single unit for the purpose of replacing F7's, F3's, and similar 1500-1800 h.p. locomotives with fewer numbers of new locomotives. This was the result of railroads having radically increased the horsepower-per-ton rating used in dispatching fast freights, which made formations of six or eight 1500-1800 h.p. units common, combined with an IRS ruling that permitted these 1500-1800 h.p. units to be written off at 15 years of age instead of 20 as ICC accounting rules required. Thus, two 2500 h.p. units, for example, could replace three 1500 h.p. F7's with horsepower to spare if eight axles of tractive power were enough to start the train and get it over the ruling grades. This process went on vigorously through the 1960's as F's were largely retired and GP7's and GP9's were downgraded to yard and local service (in turn retiring switch engines and units of minority builders). During this period, peak horsepower per unit rose from 2400 in the Alco DL640 to 2500 in the GE U25B, to 2800 in the GE U28B, to 3000 in the Alco Century 630 and in the GP40, the first 3000 h.p. B-B. In the course of this progression, locomotives formerly considered "high horsepower," such as the 2000 h.p. GP20, became intermediate horsepower at best. Also, the adhesion limits of existing B-B systems were overrun, and six-axle locomotives became the preferred high horsepower locomotives of the late 1960's and early 1970's, making the locomotives in this chapter minority types. In the GP40X we may be seeing the start of a reversal in the six-motor predominance, however.

In this book, we now consider "high horsepower" to be 3000 or greater.

EMD HIGH HORSEPOWER ROAD-SWITCHERS: 645E ENGINE, 3000 H.P. B-B

Model	A.c./d.c.	H.p.	Cyls.	Length	Truck centers	Period produced	Approx. No. of units sold		
							U.S.A.	Canada	Mexico
GP40	A.c.	3000	16	59'-2"	34'-0"	11/65-12/71	1201	24	18
GP40TC	A.c.	3000	16	65'-7"	40'-6"	11/66-12/66	None	8	None
GP40P	A.c.	3000	16	62'-8"	37'-3"	12/68	13	None	None
GP40-2	A.c.	3000	16	59'-2"	34'-0"	4/72-date	323 +[1]	275 +[1]	24 +[1]
GP40P-2	A.c.	3000	16	62'-8"	37'-3"	11/74	3	None	None

[1] Production totals are through December 31, 1977.

The preference North American railroads have for six-motor units in applications of 3000 h.p. and above started with the ACL in 1963-66 and spread rapidly, largely because of the slipperiness of high horsepower B-B's, accelerated by a spate of traction motor problems with GP40's. EMD at first suggested to the railroads that they steer away from six-axle units, pointing out that the performance curves were no different above 12 mph, but the problems with the B-B's spoke more eloquently than the performance curves. As a result, while the GP40 production totals show the result of the continuing momentum of unit-reduction orders which had previously been placed for GP20's, then GP30's, and then GP35's, the momentum soon ran down and by the time of the Dash 2 conversion, the trend was set (even though, it would turn out, the GP40-2 did eliminate many of the causes of complaint). In fact, had it not been for the heavy support of Chessie System (162 of the 323 U.S. units through 1977) and CN, which bought most of the Canadian output, the model would have been a poor seller.

GP40

The combination of B-B wheel arrangement and three large radiator fans spells GP40; regardless of whether the fat turbo stack is visible or not. Texas, Oklahoma & Eastern D-14 is an example without dynamic braking.

Marre-Mott collection, Ken Douglas.
GP40TC

The GO unit shows the current appearance of the Toronto-based GP40TC's after the rebuilding of the rear hood to silence the 500kw. head-end lighting generator.

Both GP40P

The projection at the rear of CNJ 3680 and NJDOT 4111 contains a steam generator. Even with the longer frame, the projection forced the radiators to be rearranged, SD45 style.

Both GP40-2

B&M 311 is a GP40-2 without dynamic brakes, and with the rubber-sprung Blomberg M truck. The bolted battery box cover is the only real indication that it is a Dash 2. CN 9543 is a Comfort Cab version, also lacking dynamic braking.

Marre-Mott collection, Vic Reyna.

GP40P-2

Aside from Dash 2 changes, the SP GP40P-2's differ from their CNJ counterparts mainly in having smaller fuel and water capacity, extended-range dynamic braking, and cab air conditioning.

EMD HIGH HORSEPOWER ROAD-SWITCHER: 645F ENGINE, 3500 H.P. B-B

Model	A.c./d.c.	H.p.	Cyls.	Length	Truck centers	Period produced	Approx. No. of units sold		
							U.S.A.	Canada	Mexico
GP40X[1]	A.c.	3500	16	60'-2"	35'-0"	12/77-date	37 + [2]	None[2]	None[2]

[1] Duplicates a model number used unofficially for GP40 prototype EMD No. 433A of 1965. Official model number of final production version is expected to be GP50, April 1980 or later.

[2] Production totals are through December 31, 1978.

The GP40X's are EMD's first F engines in regular production, but they are in fact prototypes for the expected "50" line due in mid 1980. Improved adhesion is supposed to be achieved through a single-axle wheelslip detection and control system, called Super Series by EMD. (GE's version, as used on five BN U30C's, is called SAWS, for Single Axle Wheelslip System.) The prototype is the ASEA system used on Swedish electric locomotives. If successful, the SS and SAWS systems could help reverse the trend toward using primarily six-axle power in road service.

GP40X

The prototype GP40X's ride on either the new HT-B truck, as illustrated by UP 9005, or the Blomberg M truck, as illustrated by AT&SF 3805 on the following page.

Larry Russell collection, George R. Cockle.

37

AT&SF 3805 rides on the familiar Blomberg M truck.   **GP40X**

EMD HIGH HORSEPOWER ROAD-SWITCHER: 645E3B ENGINE, 3500 H.P. B-B

Model	A.c./d.c.	H.p.	Cyls.	Length	Truck centers	Period produced	Approx. No. of units sold U.S.A.	Canada	Mexico
GP50	A.c.	3500	16			Introduction expected April 1980 or later			

At press time EMD was expected to begin assembly of the production model forecast by the GP40X. The GP50 is expected to differ from the GP40X prototypes in that it will not have flaring radiators because the hood has been extended to occupy the full length of the frame. If the appearance forecast proves accurate, the locomotive will resemble a GP40-2, but with the long hood extending beyond the stepwell, with passage around the hood provided for on the anti-climber.

GE HIGH HORSEPOWER ROAD-SWITCHERS: FDL16 ENGINE, 3000, 3300, 3600 H.P. B-B

Model	A.c./d.c.	H.p.	Cyls.	Length	Truck centers	Period produced	Approx. No. of units sold		
							U.S.A.	Canada	Mexico
U30B	A.c.	3000	16	60'-2"	36'-2"	12/66-3/75	291	None	None
U33B	A.c.	3300	16	60'-2"	36'-2"	9/67-8/70	137	None	None
U36B	A.c.	3600	16	60'-2"	36'-2"	1/69-12/74	125	None	None
B30-7	A.c.	3000	16	62'-2"	36'-2"	12/77-date	42 + [1]	None[1]	None[1]

[1] Production totals are through December 31, 1978 (provisional).

GE waited a year after EMD had raised 16-cylinder horsepower from 2500 to 3000 before increasing their own 16-cylinder horsepower from 2800 to 3000. Whether this delay resulted in any significant market disadvantage is hard to say. Whatever may have been lost was probably regained when GE went to 3300 and 3600 h.p. in the 16-cylinder engine, where EMD required 20 cylinders. The U33B and U36B sold almost as many units as the U30B, though only to Auto-Train, Penn Central, Rock Island, and Seaboard Coast Line. The general decline in high horsepower B-B sales affected these units. Also, most railroads were avoiding horsepowers above 3000 to save maintenance expense, which is reflected in the relatively early end-of-production dates for the U33B and U36B, and in the fact that, as of this writing, no B33-7 or B36-7 had been sold.

U30B

N&W 8510 illustrates the latter-day radiator area arrangement on U30B's. Note also that there are eight power assembly access door panels (covered by the letters RFOLK AND WES on the hood) per the eight power assemblies on the side; this feature is, of course, shared by the 3300 and 3600 h.p. models except that they also have the wide radiators, as illustrated on the facing page by Conrail U36B 2973, and Rock Island U33B 199. U36's and U33's are indistinguishable from one another.

Louis A. Marre.

40

U36B

Marre-Mott collection, J. R. Quinn.

U33B

Marre-Mott collection, Lee Hastman.

41

U30B/U28B

Closeup compares earlier and (on left) later radiator-end patterns. Version on right (on N&W U28B) was used on early U30's.

Don Dover.

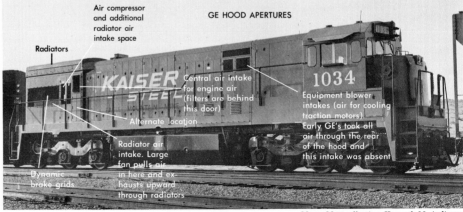

Air compressor and additional radiator air intake space

GE HOOD APERTURES

Radiators

Central air intake for engine air (filters are behind this door)

Equipment blower intakes (air for cooling traction motors). Early GE's took all air through the rear of the hood and this intake was absent

Alternate location

Radiator air intake. Large fan pulls air in here and exhausts upward through radiators

Dynamic brake grids

Marre-Mott collection, Kenneth M. Ardinger.

B30-7

Frisco 864 exhibits the step in the hood (between the letters S and C in FRISCO) which identifies the Dash 7 line and thereby distinguishes the B30-7 from the U36B and U33B. Any of the 3000 h.p., 3300 h.p., or 3600 h.p. GE B-B's may be found on ARR type B, Floating Bolster, or trade-in EMD Blomberg B trucks. Naturally, the high hood shown on N&W 8510 is not the usual arrangement but reflects the practice formerly observed on N&W and still followed on SOU of making the locomotive dual directional by eliminating the low nose. In the view of the two radiator ends on the facing page, the alternating high and low squares in the right-hand unit and the closely spaced vertical lines in a similar position on the left-hand unit are dynamic brake grids. In their absence, there is a largely unobstructed view through the radiator fan area.

MEDIUM ROAD-SWITCHERS, C-C

As in the case of B-B medium- or intermediate-horsepower road-switchers, the 2000-2300 h.p. C-C's came into being in the late 1960's as locomotive horsepower increased to the point that there was too great a gap between the maximum-horsepower locomotives being sold for unit reduction in mainline service, and switcher-size power plants. However, the C-C units did not sell as heavily as B-B's, because the C-C's low horsepower per axle made them suitable only for low-speed service. For example, when a railroad dispatches a 100-car unit coal train of 100-ton hoppers at 131 gross tons each and assigns four 3000 h.p. units to it, there is only .9 h.p. per ton to move that train. If the same train were dispatched with 2300 h.p. units, the train would have only .7 h.p. per ton. On the other hand, if B-B locomotives were assigned to the same tonnage, six units would be required to match axle count for the desired tractive effort, and six 2000 h.p. units would have the same total horsepower (12,000) as the four six-axle 3000 h.p. units. It is on such relationships that the unpopularity of the six-axle, 2000-2300 h.p. locomotive is based. With 1 h.p. per ton considered a minimum drag horsepower over most profiles and 2 h.p. per ton and above being common for hotshots, most jobs that require a six-axle unit simply need more horsepower. Those that don't, mainly certain heavy switching jobs, are still being handled by old SD7/9 power that it is not economical to replace at today's new locomotive prices, or by pairs of M.U.'ed switch engines. Thus, there has been a tendency to buy medium road-switchers primarily for low-speed heavy mineral transfer service or for hump service.

EMD MEDIUM ROAD-SWITCHERS: 645E ENGINE, 2000, 2300 H.P. C-C

Model	A.c./d.c.	H.P.	Cyls.	Length	Truck centers	Period produced	Approx. No. of units sold		
							U.S.A.	Canada	Mexico
SD38	D.c.	2000	16	65'-9.5"	40'-0"	5/67-7/71	38	None	None
SD38AC	A.c.	2000	16	65'-9.5"	40'-0"	6/71-10/71	14	1	None
SD38-2	A.c.	2000	16	68'-10"	43'-6"	11/72-date	60+[1]	7+[1]	None[1]
SD39	A.c.	2300	12	65'-9.5"	40'-0"	8/68-5/70	54	None	None
SDL39	A.c.	2300	12	55'-2"	30'-0"	3/69-11/72	10	None	None

[1] Production totals are through December 31, 1978.

Because of the nature of the six-motor, 2000-2300 h.p. locomotive as a special-application machine, sales have been scattered. Twenty months passed between the delivery of the last 567-engine version—the SD28 (only 6 were built, all in 1965, for Columbus & Greenville and Reserve Mining)—and the first SD38. It was another 13 months between the last SD38 delivery and the first SD38-2, and from 1975 to date only two units have been built. The other 65 units were built between November 1972 and the end of 1975, 33 in 1975 alone. The biggest customer for the units have been the U.S. steel roads with their slow road speeds. For example, 30 of the 60 U.S. SD38-2's went to B&LE, EJ&E, and DM&IR. The majority of the remaining sales have been for hump

Continued

B&LE SD38AC 869, equipped with dynamic brakes and paper air filters, is visually indistinguishable from DC SD38's. The SD38 and SD38AC are distinguished from the few (six) SD28's by having 11 instead of 10 handrail stanchions along the long hood, due to the longer underframe. They are distinguishable from SD39's by the absence of the fat turbocharger stack, having instead two small stacks in line ahead of and behind the dynamic brake hatch, if any. The paper air-filter box mounting as on B&LE 869 is inconsistent with the turbo stack placement, and therefore this is shown to be an SD38. The quick distinction for SD38's, SD39's, and SD38-2's from similar SD40 and SD40-2 models is that the latter have three large radiator fans instead of two; the SD35 has two large fans with a small one between them. The most dependable distinction for SD38-2's is the bolt-on instead of latched battery box cover, as found on U.S.-built BC Hydro SD38-2 382 (following page).

Marre-Mott collection, Ken Douglas.

locomotives, as on SP, L&N, C&NW, PC/CR, and DT&I. During the last year of SD38 production, the model was offered with a.c. instead of d.c. transmission as an option, and all but DT&I's last two SD38's were built as a.c. thereafter. When the SD39 was introduced, EMD apparently intended that it replace the SD38 in the catalog, but like the GP39 in relation to the GP38, EMD found that many roads preferred to avoid the turbocharger where possible. Although the sales of the SD39 were respectable compared to its catalog mate, the SD38 (54 versus 53 units), when the Dash 2 conversion was made on January 1, 1972, no SD39-2 was listed in the catalog. EMD emphasized that it would continue to build units to customer order, but unlike the GP39-2, no such customer demand for an SD39-2 has developed as of this writing, although it could happen, for the same reason GP39-2 demand developed.

The SDL39 is one of the most interesting of the special-application locomotives developed by EMD. Milwaukee Road wanted to replace its Alco RSC2's,

SD38-2

Like B&LE 869 (previous page), BC Hydro 382 has paper air filters, which are inconsistent in this mounting with a turbocharger. However, paper air filters are an option and therefore should not be depended on as a spotting feature for SD38's and SD38-2's.

Marre-Mott collection, Larry Russell.

whose mere 237,000 lbs. were spread over six axles (only 19.75 tons per axle, versus the 30 tons per axle more typical of U.S. road units). The answer was the SDL39. By shortening the frame and using specially lightened (export) truck frames, EMD was able to hold the weight of these units to 250,000 lbs. on six axles (20.8 tons per axle) and stay within the rail and bridge load limits of the light branches where the RSC2's had been operating. The 10 SDL39's were built in two batches, five in 1969 and five late in 1972 after all other non-Dash

2 production had long since ceased. A major feature that EMD used to reduce the weight of the locomotive was the 12-cylinder turbocharged prime mover instead of the heavier 16-cylinder Roots blower version found on SD38's. Very seldom is the weight of a prime mover a significant consideration in U.S. diesel locomotives because there is usually a need to ballast for tractive power anyway. (The only exception is where it is desirable to stay within the load limits of shop cranes used for lifting out engines.)

Marre-Mott collection, Vic Reyna.

Marre-Mott collection, Ken Douglas.

SP 5316 is a heavily-equipped SD39 having extended-range dynamic braking. Illinois Terminal 2305 is a stripped version having few options applied. On both, the turbocharger stack is visible on the roof line just behind the dust evacuator dome of the inertial air filter. Interestingly, SP owns both SD39's and SD38-2's.

Both SD39

W. S. Kuba.

Note the unique trucks and the short frame (just nine handrail stanchions along the long hood) which are distinguishing features of the SDL39.

SDL39

GE MEDIUM ROAD-SWITCHERS: FDL12 ENGINE, 2250 H.P. B-B

Model	A.c./d.c.	H.p.	Cyls.	Length	Truck centers	Period produced	Approx. No. of units sold		
							U.S.A.	Canada	Mexico
U23C	D.c.	2250	12	67'-3"	40'-11"	3/68-9/70	53	None	None

The U23C shared with equivalent EMD models the patchy, special-purpose ordering which characterizes these low-horsepower-per-axle locomotives. Although a C23-7 is in GE's current catalog, none had been ordered as of this writing. LS&I 2300-2304, BN 5200-5208 (ex-CB&Q 460-468), AT&SF 7500-7519, and Conrail 6700-6718 (ex-PC same number) were the U23C's sold.

U23C

As with other GE's, the number of cylinders in the U23C engine is given away by having six door panels for power assembly access where the letters &IRR appear on LS&I 2300. Note the fairing at the hood top where the radiator housing joins. This feature was squared off on all GE U-series locomotives after September 1968.

Ken Douglas.

HIGH HORSEPOWER ROAD-SWITCHERS, C-C

EMD's introduction of the 20-cylinder 645 engine in 1965 carried the horsepower race (which had been in progress among the builders since 1959) to the 3600 h.p. level. To that point, the railroads had given every indication that they wanted more and more horsepower per unit to get the maximum unit-reduction economies in retiring power in the 1500-1800 h.p. range. GE and Alco were able to follow the increase to 3600 h.p. in their 16-cylinder engines, and for a while it seemed that a lively race to higher horsepowers would ensue, with EMD experimenting with seven 4200 h.p. machines (SD45X's) and MLW with one short-lived 4000 h.p. unit (M640). However, railroads experienced heavy maintenance expenditures with the 3300-3600 h.p. locomotives, and a preference for 3000 h.p. designs soon made itself felt on the order books of the early 1970's. This, along with the exit of Alco from the market place, cooled the competition and resulted in an era of builders concentrating on improved reliability rather than radical new designs. During this era, railroads also shifted their preference from B-B to C-C units because of adhesion and traction-motor-maintenance problems with B-B units in this power range. A revitalization of coal traffic in many areas of the country further accentuated the trend to C-C's, particularly the 3000 h.p. models.

EMD HIGH HORSEPOWER ROAD-SWITCHERS: 645E ENGINE, 3000 H.P. C-C

Model	A.c./d.c.	H.p.	Cyls.	Length	Truck centers	Period produced	Approx. No. of units sold		
							U.S.A.	Canada	Mexico
SD40	A.c.	3000	16	65'-9.5"[1]	40'-0"	1/66-7/72	865	330	62
SD40A	A.c.	3000	16	70'-8"	45'-0"	8/69-1/70	18	None	None
SDP40	A.c.	3000	16	65'-8"	40'-0"	6/66-5/70	6	None	14
SD40-2	A.c.	3000	16	68'-10"	43'-6"	1/72-date	1852+[2]	467+[2]	72+[2]
SD40-2SS	A.c.	3000	16	68'-10"	43'-6"	3/78-date	5+[2]	None[2]	None[2]
SD40T-2	A.c.	3000	16	68'-10"	43'-6"	6/74-date	109+[2]	None[2]	None[2]

[1] The standard SD40/SD45 underframe was slightly revised in 1968 to this dimension from 65'-8", with no change in truck centers.
[2] Production totals are through December 31, 1978.

Railroads at first were tentative in their ordering of SD40's as opposed to the contemporary SD45 model; they had been conditioned by the horsepower race to seek the highest horsepower per unit to maximize the benefits of unit reduction. However, when railroads experienced high maintenance expenses for a relatively minor advance in horsepower per unit, they returned to the 16-cylinder models, making the SD40-2 practically the standard locomotive of the late 1970's. Along the way, EMD produced a few variations that were significant enough to merit their own model numbers. The first was the SDP40, built only for Great Northern and National Railways of Mexico to replace aging F-type power in transcontinental passenger service. BN converted the ex-GN

Continued

SD40

KCS 632 is an SD40 equipped with extended-range dynamic brake. The SD40 identification feature is three closely-spaced radiator fans of equal size above vertical radiators. The otherwise-similar SD35 has two large fans flanking a small one.

Louis A. Marre.

units to freight service when Amtrak was created, and thereafter they functioned the same as any other SD40. The next variation was the SD40A, an Illinois Central (later Illinois Central Gulf) special order in which SD40 machinery was used with the longer underframe of an SDP45 to provide enlarged fuel tank capacity. These 18 units were delivered in two orders, one in 1969 and one in 1970. The SD40-2 became the successor of the SD40 in January 1972; however, five SD40's were delivered to Detroit Edison in 1972 at their request to maintain standardization in their small fleet. The main functional change in the SD40-2 is the modular electronic control system and the HT-C (high traction) truck. However, Conrail SD40-2's purchased after formation of that railroad April 1, 1976, have Flexicoil trucks owing to the controversy which surrounded the HT-C truck during 1976-77. The first major variation in the SD40-2 was the SD40T-2, purchased only by Southern Pacific and Denver & Rio Grande Western. The variation originated on the SP with

SD45T's, and is represented on the SD40T-2 by a low air intake with fans mounted beneath the radiators, which are set horizontally in the rear of the hood. The purpose of this change was to enable locomotives to gather cooler air from nearer track level while passing through tunnels and snowsheds on heavy grades. Rear units in consists on heavy grades tend to trip their hot engine shutdowns in tunnels as units ahead of them heat the air. The next modification to be introduced, in 1975, was the Comfort Cab or Safety Cab on SD40-2's built for Canadian National. This did not result in a new model number, but the units are sometimes referred to as SD40-2(W) for "wide nose." Finally, the SD40-2SS appeared in 1978 as a test of the Super Series electrical system in six-motor units. BN 7049-7053 were the only such units as of this writing; the change requires a larger alternator but causes no external difference in the locomotive.

SD40

GTW 5902 is an SD40 not equipped with dynamic braking.

Louis A. Marre.

Louis A. Marre.

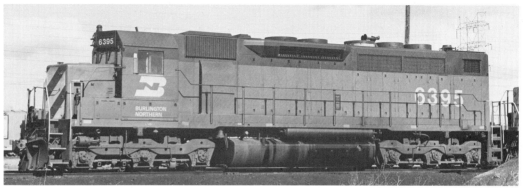

Marre-Mott collection, James B. Holder.

BN 6395 and NdeM 8524 represent the only two orders for the SDP40. All machinery is located forward of the usual SD40 position to provide room for the steam generator compartment at the rear, and by so doing, no departure from the standard SD40/SD45 underframe length was needed (see insert of rear end of BN 1976).

Both SDP40

Marre-Mott collection, Larry Russell.

Burdell Bulgrin.

SD40A

The SD40A is SD40 machinery resting on an SDP45 frame to provide room between the trucks for larger fuel capacity. Only Illinois Central Gulf ordered them.

SD40-2

CP 5789 is a conventional SD40-2 equipped with dynamic braking but without the enlarged anti-climber which has been common on SD40-2 orders since 1973. The three-lens class lights and high bell mounting, with headlight in the short hood, are unique Canadian features, along with the pilot and ditch lights. CR 6396 (facing page) displays the anti-climber option, as well as the use of Flexicoil instead of HT-C trucks, unique to Conrail.

Marre-Mott collection, Larry Russell.

Marre-Mott collection, Jack Armstrong.

SD40-2

UP 8009 is an SD40-2 having an extended nose used to house RC equipment. Extended-nose units have been built for both SP and UP. HT-C truck spotting features: six instead of four perforations in the sideframe and shock absorber over the center axle.

SD40T-2

SP 8492 is an SD40T-2. The modified radiator extends the rear hood about three feet onto the lengthy rear platform. SD40T-2's are distinguished from SD45T-2's by having two radiator fan access doors under the radiators (and above the air intake), as opposed to three doors on the SD45T-2.

Marre-Mott collection, J. R. Quinn.

Marre-Mott collection, Vic Reyna.

CN 5304 illustrates the safety cab version of the SD40-2; CN's are the only SD40-2's with this type of cab.

Marre-Mott collection, Larry Russell.

SD40-2

EMD HIGH HORSEPOWER ROAD-SWITCHERS: 645E ENGINE, 3600, 4200 H.P. C-C

Model	A.c./d.c.	H.p.	Cyls.	Length	Truck centers	Period produced	Approx. No. of units sold		
							U.S.A.	Canada	Mexico
SD45	A.c.	3600	20	65'-9.5"[1]	40'-0"	2/65-12/71	1260	None	None
SDP45	A.c.	3600	20	70'-8"	45'-0"	5/67-8/70	52	None	None
SD45X	A.c.	4200	20	70'-8"	45'-0"	6/70-2/71	7	None	None
SD45-2	A.c.	3600	20	68'-10"	43'-6"	5/72-9/74[2]	136	None	None
SD45T-2	A.c.	3600	20	68'-10"	43'-6"	2/72-6/75[2]	247	None	None

[1] The standard SD40/SD45 underframe was slightly revised in 1968 to this dimension from 65'-8" with no change in truck centers.

[2] Because there has been no production since the dates shown, production is shown as if completed. However, it appears nothing would prevent more SD45-2's or SD45T-2's from being made if ordered.

The SD45, as the top of the horsepower line at EMD, dominated sales for the first few years after its introduction, but problems with maintenance costs of the 20-cylinder engine and the big radiators soon caused railroads to question the value of the extra 600 h.p. per unit as compared with the SD40. The Dash 2 conversion of 1972, in addition to the modular electronics and HT-C truck common to the SD40's, addressed the radiator problem by eliminating the angular mounting. Nonetheless, most railroads had already made their decision, and only AT&SF, Clinchfield, EL (now Conrail) and SCL ordered SD45-2's, while the Southern Pacific/Cotton Belt accounted for all of the "tunnel" version, the SD45T-2, the purpose of which is explained in relation to

SD45

D&RGW 5324 illustrates an SD45 with extended-range dynamic braking; C&NW 911 (facing page) is an SD45 with no dynamic braking, the only road so specifying. The distinctive feature of the SD45 is its flared radiator mounting with three screened air inlets to a side (behind which a bank of four radiator cores is mounted).

58

the SD40T-2. The SDP45 was originally developed to provide a passenger locomotive for replacing F-type power in transcontinental service, but only Great Northern (now BN) and Southern Pacific bought them for this purpose. A majority of the units built, 34, went to EL strictly as freight power, with the long underframe used only to provide added fuel capacity (for the same reason, the same underframe was also used to make the IC SD40A).

The SD45X, six of which wound up on SP's rosters and one of which was retained by EMD as a test bed, was most important as the pioneer of the Dash 2 modifications, especially the HT-C truck. It too rode on an SDP45 frame. The experimental high horsepower was not, for the time being, pursued since railroads were showing a lack of interest in paying the price that higher unit horsepower demanded in terms of maintenance, as reflected in the fall-off of SD45 sales.

Marre-Mott collection, Lee Hastman.

SD45

Marre-Mott collection, Don Dover.

Marre-Mott collection, Vic Reyna.

Because of the combination of the 20-cylinder engine with the steam generator compartment, a five-foot longer frame was needed for the SDP45 compared to the SD40/SD45. The rear views show, on SP 3205, the squared-off end housing the steam generator on the passenger version of this model, while the rear end photo of EL 3641 shows the beveled end on the EL (now Conrail) freight version which was purchased to use the longer frame for added fuel capacity.

All SDP45

Louis A. Marre.

SD45X

EMD 4202 exhibits the quickest identifying feature of the SD45X, the four large radiator fans. Note also the HT-C trucks.

Marre-Mott collection, Kenneth M. Ardinger.

SD45-2

AT&SF 5698 illustrates the primary SD45-2 identification features: the long radiator area with three widely-spaced fans and the lack of long end platforms, all on an HT-C truck locomotive. These provide the easiest distinction from the otherwise-similar SD40-2, which rides the same-length underframe. AT&SF 5698 has a cab air conditioner, the box on the cab roof.

Marre-Mott collection, Vic Reyna.

Both photos, Louis A. Marre.

SD45T-2

SP 9204 from the front, and SP 9204 from the rear exhibit the identifying low air intake and absence of visible radiator fans on the tunnel motor SD45's. The most visible distinction from the otherwise similar SD40T-2's is that because of the 20-cylinder engine, the locomotive fully occupies the standard SD40-2/SD45-2 underframe without leaving the big front and back porches seen on the 16-cylinder model, and there are three radiator fan access doors on the SD45T-2 instead of two on the SD40T-2.

EMD HIGH HORSEPOWER ROAD-SWITCHERS: 645E3B ENGINE, 3500 H.P. C-C

Model	A.c./d.c.	H.p.	Cyls.	Length	Truck centers	Period produced	Approx. No. of units sold		
							U.S.A.	Canada	Mexico
SD50	A.c.	3500	16				Introduction expected in 1980		

At press time EMD was expected to place into production a Super Series replacement for the SD40-2, which would probably also officially retire the SD45-2 from the catalog. Preliminary information on the appearance of this locomotive indicates that it will be very similar to the SD45-2, but as on the GP50, the hood would be extended beyond the stepwells with passage around the hood provided for on the anti-climbers.

GE HIGH HORSEPOWER ROAD-SWITCHERS: FDL16 ENGINE, 3000, 3300, 3430, 3600 H.P. C-C

Model	A.c./d.c.	H.p.	Cyls.	Length	Truck centers	Period produced	Approx. No. of units sold		
							U.S.A.	Canada	Mexico
U30C	A.c.	3000	16	67'-3"	40'-11"	1/67-9/76	592	None	8
U33C	A.c.	3300	16	67'-3"	40'-11"	1/68-1/75	375	None	None
U34CH	A.c.	3430	16	67'-3"	40'-11"	11/70-1/73	32	None	None
U36C	A.c.	3600	16	67'-3"	40'-11"	10/71-4/75	124	None	94
U36CG	A.c.	3600	16	67'-3"	40'-11"	4/74-5/74	None	None	20
C30-7	A.c.	3000	16	67'-3"	40'-11"	9/76-date	246 + [1]	None[1]	None[1]

[1] Production totals are through December 31, 1978 (preliminary).

The U30C was an evolutionary rerating of the U28C, and the first U30C's were visually indistinguishable from late U28C's. The U33C and U36C were essentially the same locomotive as the U30C, but with advanced fuel rate and a larger radiator area. In the case of the U36C, steel-capped pistons were used. The ability to go to 3600 h.p. in 16 cylinders gave GE a sales point for a brief season, as compared to EMD's 20-cylinder locomotives, but this advantage melted away as railroads concluded that none of the locomotives over 3000 h.p. were worth the extra maintenance expense. Although no C33-7 or C36-7 has been ordered as of this writing, they are in the catalog and could appear. All advance indications are that they would be identical in appearance to the

Continued

U30C

Kaiser Steel 1030 represents the first style of U30C carbody after the U28C style, with the radiator end of the hood wider than the rest and a small fairing piece at the top of the hood at radiator level. Rock Island 4598 on the following page shows the later version (after September 1978) with this small fairing piece missing. On the Kaiser unit note that the most-forward air intake on the radiator bulge is high, whereas on the RI unit it is low. These position variations formerly depended on the type of air filter used, but this is no longer a consistent indication.

Joe McMillan.

C30-7. The U34CH is a U36C fitted with a train-lighting alternator, giving a nominal rating of 3430 h.p., although this varies downward depending on the lighting demand of the train. At one time there was a plan to have GE buy back a C&NW U30C to convert to a thirty-third U34CH, because the changed layout of the 7-series locomotives does not leave room for a train-lighting alternator (which occupied the "steam generator room" behind the cab on the U-series engines). On the other hand, the U36CG was simply a case of putting a steam generator in this compartment.

Louis A. Marre.

U30C

Marre-Mott collection, Kenneth M. Ardinger.

U33C

BN 5761 illustrates that the U33C is identical to the U30C except for the wider radiator area. The numerals "61" and the ACI label on the side of the hood extend across the eight power asembly access door panels. Eight doors indicate a 16-cylinder engine; the 12-cylinder models have six of these high door panels.

U36C

AT&SF 8700 is a U36C, visually indistinguishable from the U33C. The only U36C's are AT&SF 8700-8799, CRR 3600-3606 (to SCL 2125-2131), EL 3316-3328 (to Conrail 6587-6599), MILW 8500-8503, NdeM 8900-8937, 8958-8986, 9300-9316 (8938-8957 are U36CG's), and Pacifico 409-418.

Marre-Mott collection, J. R. Quinn.

U36CG

NdeM 8945 is a U36CG, which is simply a U36C with a steam generator occupying the compartment provided for this purpose on all U-series C-C's. Note the housing for steam generator vents on the roof behind the cab.

Marre-Mott collection, Keith E. Ardinger.

C30-7

BN 5509 illustrates the identifying feature of the C30-7, the step in the hood between the numerals "55" and "09". Despite being 3000 h.p., the C30-7's have the wide radiator area previously identified with 3300 and 3600 h.p. units.

Gordon B. Mott.

U34CH

EL-New Jersey DOT 3368 illustrates the U34CH, which preceded U36C production by a year, although mechanically the engine was a forecast of the steel-capped pistons used to make the 3600 h.p.-for-traction rating practical. The train lighting alternator occupies the space behind the cab.

Marre-Mott collection, W. J. Brennan.

Model	A.c./d.c.	H.p.	Cyls.	Length	Truck centers	Period produced	Approx. No. of units sold U.S.A.	Canada	Mexico
M630	A.c.	3000	16	69'-6"	41'-10"	11/69-11/73	None	55	20
M636	A.c.	3600	16	69'-6"	41'-10"	11/69-4/75	None	95	16

Although these units are shown as if production were completed, it is possible more will be ordered. These models are MLW versions of the Alco Century 630 and Century 636 with slight engineering changes.

M630

The M630 and M636 are distinguished from the Century equivalents (C630, C636) by the faired after-cooler box which appears at the hood top behind the cab. This box is not faired on the Centuries. The M630 is distinguished from the M636 by the fairing where the radiator joins the long hood. The M636 is squared off at this point.

Norm Herbert.

M636

CP 4717 illustrates an M636 for comparison of the radiator area. Both CP 4553 (facing page) and 4717 ride on the MLW truck which resembles the GE floating-bolster truck.

Both photos, Marre-Mott collection, Larry Russell.

M630

BCOL 727 illustrates the M630 in the Comfort Cab or Safety Cab version, found only on BCOL.

COWL UNITS

The term "cowl" has been applied to locomotives having a non-structural full-width covering of their machinery, instead of a hood. The cowl units were different from the old "carbody" locomotives such as the EMD FT, F3, F7, and F9. As carbody implies, an F unit was built like a passenger car housing machinery. Its sides and roof were structural, somewhat like a truss bridge, whereas the new cowl units use the underframe for carrying the machinery load, just like a road-switcher. The cowl is simply a weather shelter. The original cowl units, the AT&SF FP45's, were ordered to provide a more acceptable appearance for use on premier passenger trains than a road-switcher body would have provided. Additional reasons given were that such a locomotive would offer less air resistance and could be worked on en route at passenger speeds. Some may question whether the angular EMD styling accomplished the esthetic purposes. The cowl units did, however, offer a cab that was considerably more weather-tight in winter, and not subject to having the cab doors sealed shut by snow and ice. Hence, Great Northern and successor Burlington Northern became a purchaser after AT&SF. Although the cowling does permit the engine to be looked over on the road, not much of that is done anymore. Further, cowled locomotives are more difficult to work on in the shop than hood units, so the cowl idea quickly died away, its demise hastened by the proportionately higher maintenance requirements of the EMD 20-cylinder engine and its radiator arrangement. There are exceptions: Amtrak and some commuter authorities, still concerned with appearance, have continued to order 16-cylinder cowl locomotives. Interestingly, the generous cabs of the cowl units are a severable concept from the cowl itself—witness the DD40AX of the following chapter—and that part of the idea, embodied in the Canadian Comfort or Safety Cab and in the GE Quarters Cab, lives on.

EMD COWL UNITS, 645E ENGINE, 3000, 3600 H.P. C-C

Model	A.c./d.c.	H.p.	Cyls.	Length	Truck centers	Period produced	Approx. No. of units sold		
							U.S.A.	Canada	Mexico
F45	A.c.	3600	20	67'-5.5"	41'-8"	6/68-5/71	86	None	None
FP45	A.c.	3600	20	72'-4"¹	45'-0"	12/67-12/68	14	None	None
SDP40F	A.c.	3000	16	72'-4"	46'-0"	6/73-8/74	150	None	None
F40C	A.c.	3200	16	68'-10"	43'-6"	3/74-5/74	15	None	None

¹ MILW FP45's are 70'-8"

The original cowl units were the FP45's and F45's for Santa Fe. Milwaukee subsequently ordered FP45's and Great Northern, and later BN, ordered F45's. The FP45's were designed such that they would be suitable as freight locomotives if no longer needed for passenger service, and they were so converted after Amtrak began in May 1971. When Amtrak decided to order its first new power, the FP45 was a logical choice, and so they bought the SDP40F, which was, in effect, a 16-cylinder Dash 2 version of the FP45 riding on the Dash 2 HT-C trucks. It was a consideration that these engines could be readily converted to freight service if Amtrak folded, but in addition, the Great Northern, Southern Pacific, and Santa Fe had already demonstrated that high-horse-

Continued

F45

BN 6622 illustrates the identifying characteristics of the F45 compared to the FP45: the lack of any space between the radiator and the rear of the cowl. The FP45 has space here representing the length of the steam generator platform.

Gordon B. Mott.

power C-C's could replace F's in passenger service with unit reduction, and Amtrak was merely following previously accepted railroad practice. During the same period, two Chicago area commuter agencies, the North Suburban Mass Transit District and the Northwest Suburban Mass Transit District, ordered 15 (2 and 13 units respectively) F40C's, which in principle was an SDP40F except that the F40C was shorter because it carried a 500 kw train lighting/heating alternator rather than the more space-consuming steam generators found on SDP40F's. Soon after delivery, the SDP40F's were involved in a number of derailments which had similar characteristics. In each of these derailments (eventually about 10 fit the pattern) the train was entering a curve of about 2 degrees at a speed between 40 and 60 mph, and the trailing truck of the trailing unit, or the lead truck of the baggage car behind, derailed due to lateral force turning rail. Usually a small track perturbation was present, but well within FRA limits for Class 4 track. Concurrent to these derailment episodes, the SDP40F was brought under attack by the Brotherhood of Locomotive Engineers as a possibly unsafe locomotive because of heavy yaw characteristics under normal track conditions. However, little correlation could be established between the yaw condition and the derailments.

The culminating events were a derailment on December 16, 1976, at Ralston, Nebr., on Burlington Northern, which led to the removal of the SDP40F from all BN-operated Amtrak trains (they later returned under a 40 mph restriction for all curves of 2 degrees and over) and a similar derailment 30 days later on the L&N at Newcastle, Ala., which caused the 40 mph speed restriction to be made national by the FRA (it was later lifted on roads with Class 5 track). At this point, Amtrak decided there was something wrong with the locomotives, even though extensive testing could not pinpoint the cause. Unique to the SDP40F were its hollow-bolster trucks (which slightly skewed the center of rotation on the already off-center HT-C truck) and its truck-center spacing and carbody weight distribution. There was speculation that some kind of harmonic action was set up, either in the hollow-bolster truck alone or in conjunction with the locomotive body yaw and/or baggage car yaw, that led to the destructive lateral force observed in the derailments.

Nothing had been proven as of this writing, but the uncertainty led to some immediate results. First, Amtrak decided to use the SDP40F's as trades for F40PH's, which they would use even for transcontinental runs. (The SDP40F was designed to have its skid-mounted steam generators replaced by skid-mounted engine/alternator sets as Amtrak electrified its heating and lighting systems; it was decided that the heating/lighting alternators of the F40PH's would be used instead). Thus, by early 1979 more than half the SDP40F's had already been scrapped before reaching their fifth birthday. Secondly, transit districts began buying F40PH's, leaving the F40C a one-time orphan although its trucks and geometry are almost exactly that of the well-proven SD40-2 and it probably should not have been tarred with the same brush as the SDP40F. Despite a tendency to seek somebody to blame, there is no evidence that EMD, Amtrak, or the operating railroads should have foreseen the SDP40F's problems, because the locomotive embodied what seemed to be well-engineered components with ample precedents in industry practice. What is important is that appropriate action was taken to protect the public as soon as the problem was perceived, and what is unfortunate is that the research efforts so far have not explained what happened.

MILW 1, an FP45, illustrates the space between the radiators and the rear end of the cowl, which distinguishes this model from the F45.

FP45

Both SDP40F

The first 40 SDP40F's had the same pointed nose as the F45's and FP45's, as illustrated by Amtrak 521. The remaining units had a flattened nose which simplified sheet metal work, as shown by Amtrak 597. All SDP40F's lacked the nose platform found on F45's and FP45's, and SDP40F's have the HT-C truck.

Marre-Mott collection, J. R. Quinn.

F40C

The F40C, illustrated by Northwest Suburban Mass Transit District 48, is most readily distinguished by its jalousie side panels. Otherwise, the units have HT-C trucks and the nose style of the second-order SDP40F's. Its 3200 h.p. rating was provided to give traction reserve when up to 700 h.p. was drawn off for train heating and lighting requirements.

EMD COWL UNITS, 645E ENGINE, 3000 H.P. B-B

Model	A.c./d.c.	H.p.	Cyls.	Length	Truck centers	Period produced	Approx. No. of units sold		
							U.S.A.	Canada	Mexico
F40PH	A.c.	3000/3200	16	56'-2"	33'-0"	3/76-date	173 + [1]	6 + [1]	None

[1] Production totals are through December 31, 1978.

When the F40PH was introduced it was intended for short-haul and commuter trains heated by a head-end alternator instead of steam, and a 500 kw heating/lighting alternator was provided that would draw off a maximum of 710 h.p. from the traction alternator. When the F40PH supplanted the SDP40F as the prospective power for transcontinental Superliner trains, Amtrak's new electrically heated and lighted double-deck cars intended for long-distance Western services, it was necessary to modify the F40PH with an 800 kw heating/lighting alternator and equip them with an 1800-gallon fuel tank instead of the earlier 1200 gallons. The first non-Amtrak order was for Chicago's RTA (Regional Transit Authority) who specified that they wanted the same rating from the 16-645E powerplant as provided on the NWSMTD/NSMTD F40C's—3200 h.p. This is simply a matter of fuel rack settings; in fact, many Amtrak F40PH's on load test are found to be set at well over 3000 h.p. When operated in multiple, only one F40PH at a time can furnish head-end power for train heating and lighting so that all 3000-plus horsepower of the other unit(s) is available for traction.

Both F40PH

Amtrak 207 is from the original order (200-229). Its fuel tank is located next to the rear truck. In later units the tank is near the front truck and is larger, as on Amtrak 278 on the facing page.

Marre-Mott collection, Jack Armstrong.

Gordon B. Mott.

GE COWL UNITS, FDL16 ENGINE, 3000 H.P. C-C

Model	A.c./d.c.	H.p.	Cyls.	Length	Truck centers	Period produced	Approx. No. of units sold		
							U.S.A.	Canada	Mexico
U30CG	A.c.	3000	16	67'-3"	40'-11"	11/67	6	None	None
P30CH	A.c.	3000	16	72'-4"	46'-0"	8/75-1/76	25	None	None

AT&SF specified a full-width body for its new passenger locomotives from GE and well as EMD. Both builders delivered their versions the same month, bringing the cowl unit into the North American railroad scene. The GE entry was called the U30CG, and unlike the FP45, did not require a frame longer than those on GE's standard 3000 h.p. C-C's. This was because GE had always provided a steam generator compartment behind the cab on all domestic C-C U-series locomotives, whether it was used as such or not (this space was eliminated on the Dash 7 series locomotives). Santa Fe had previously ordered U28CG's which did not have the cowl; the U30CG simply repeated the idea mechanically, but with a full-width body.

Marre-Mott collection, J. R. Quinn.

Marre-Mott collection, Gordon B. Mott.

P30CH

Amtrak 724 illustrates the front and side of the P30CH, with its unusual orientation of the central air intakes to the rear of the radiator intakes. The rear view of Amtrak 721 illustrates the ventilation for the auxiliary heating/lighting engine.

The P30CH, on the other hand, was a departure in that it provided an electric heating/lighting auxiliary engine/generator set at the rear of the locomotive, instead of a steam generator. Originally, it was intended that these locomotives would start life on electrically heated and lighted Amfleet trains and then graduate to the long-distance electric heat/light Superliner trains when they were delivered. However, in the wake of the SDP40F derail-ment problems and similar problems with the GE E60 electrics, the F40PH got the nod for the transcontinental assignments, and the P30CH's became orphans on the roster. The P30CH's were not suitable for trade-in on F40PH's as the SDP40F's were, and were undesired for long-term Amfleet service because of Amtrak's suspicion of six-motor power. It seemed likely that Amtrak would try to sell the P30CH's as freight locomotives when it became possible to do so.

Both photos, Marre-Mott collection, Louis A. Marre.

U30CG

Santa Fe 8004 illustrates the U30CG in the AT&SF freight colors (blue and yellow). An air intake for the steam generator is located in the compartment behind the cab. The central air intake for the prime mover is concealed behind the large louvers under the radiator air intake. Note that the fuel and water tanks have now been combined (the filler receptacle under "t" in "Santa Fe" has been removed).

DUAL-ENGINE FREIGHT LOCOMOTIVES

The dual-engine freight locomotive was a concept revived in the 1960's by D. S. Neuhart, then Chief Mechanical Officer of the Union Pacific. Naturally, there was a precedent for such locomotives, primarily the Baldwin Centipede, but the idea had not been in favor for many years when Neuhart promoted it. His concept was that many expenses of a locomotive occur just because it is a unit, and that dual-engine power would justify its higher initial cost (as a special order item) by lower maintenance costs. Although this did not prove to be the case, the attempt to find out provided interesting variety to the locomotive scene. The first of the Neuhart dual-engine locomotives were the EMD DD35B and GE U50 of 1963. These locomotives were almost literally "two of everything on a raft" with little new engineering except of underframes, and,

of course, of the colossal EMD D truck (the B+B-B+B GE's rode on traded-in span-bolster sets of AAR type B road trucks from older GE turbines). The second generation of dual-engine power was more highly engineered, as reflected in the DD40AX and U50C. The DD40AX in particular reflected the concerted effort of UP to get EMD to systematize its control circuits with modularization, and as a result it became a preview of the Dash 2 modular electronics. In like fashion a decade earlier, UP's experimental "Omaha GP20's" had pushed EMD into turbocharging and forecast EMD's regular model GP20. In the end, though, such special engineering was more than even UP felt it could afford, and after the 1969 orders were delivered (through 1971 in the case of GE), UP returned to ordering off-the-shelf models.

EMD DUAL-ENGINE FREIGHT LOCOMOTIVE, 6600 H.P. D-D

Model	A.c./d.c.	H.p.	Cyls.	Length	Truck centers	Period produced	Approx. No. of units sold		
							U.S.A.	Canada	Mexico
DD40AX	A.c.	6600	(2)16	98'-5"	65'-0"	4/69-9/71	47	None	None

The DD40AX was built to Union Pacific special order and is also known as the "Centennial" type in honor of the 100th anniversary in 1969 of the Golden Spike ceremony at Promontory, Utah. Internally, the DD40AX employs modular electronics that later became standard on the Dash 2 line. The units were technically successful but did not show sufficient operating economies over off-the-shelf locomotives to justify their special-order cost, and subsequent UP orders have been for standard models, chiefly SD40-2's.

Marre-Mott collection, J. R. Quinn.

DD40AX

UP 6916 illustrates the unmistakable features of the DD40AX, with its cowl-style cab, lengthy hood with flared radiators, and D trucks. The bin at the edge of the underframe (covering part of the second "I" in PACIFIC) is the sandbox for the left rear wheels. The tank holds 8280 gallons, compared to 4000 on comparable single-engine C-C's.

GE DUAL-ENGINE FREIGHT LOCOMOTIVE, 5000 H.P. C-C

Model	A.c./d.c.	H.p.	Cyls.	Length	Truck centers	Period produced	Approx. No. of units sold		
							U.S.A.	Canada	Mexico
U50C	A.c.	5000	(2)12	79'-0"	50'-2"	9/69-11/71	40	None	None

The U50C was the GE contemporary to the EMD DD40AX and was likewise a special order for Union Pacific, but differed in concept in that the locomotive used the trucks from traded-in GE 8500 h.p. two-unit turbine locomotives. GE had been using modular electronics since the introduction of the U25B in 1960 and therefore that feature was not a novelty, as with the DD40AX. The cab was a carry-over from the earlier U50, but the 5000 h.p. rating was derived from two 12-cylinder engines instead of two 16-cylinder engines on the U50. The locomotives proved to be technically unsuccessful and were withdrawn from service when less than 10 years old.

U50C

The main identifying features of the U50C are its C-C trucks and centered "wingspan" radiator arrangement. The generator ends of the engines point outward from the central radiator area, a layout shared with the other UP dual-engine freight locomotives.

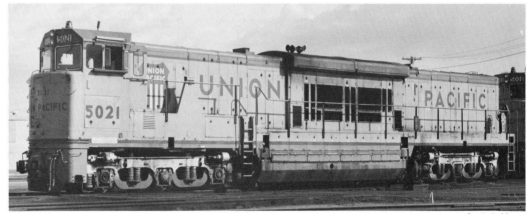

Louis A. Marre.

LIGHTWEIGHT-TRAIN POWER CARS

About once every 20 years, after the generation which remembers why articulated lightweight trains are undesirable retires, along comes another generation that is captivated by the engineering advantages of greatly reduced train weight made possible by reducing the buffing requirements of cars. Lightweight trains can achieve high speed on relatively little horsepower, and often have low centers of gravity and special suspensions for higher-than-normal curve-negotiation speeds. Such trains have been successful in Europe because of high frequency of scheduling, but in the U.S., where trains are few, the expected passenger load fluctuates enough to make the fixed consists of lightweight trains awkward, and they also tend to be expensive to maintain. Amtrak and VIA Rail Canada are giving the idea another turn, however.

UNITED AIRCRAFT, ANF-FRANGECO, ROHR, MLW, WERKSPOOR-UTRECHT LIGHTWEIGHT-TRAIN POWER CARS

Builder	Trans.	H.p.	Cyls.	Length	Truck centers	Period produced	Approx. No. of units sold		
							U.S.A.	Canada	Mexico
UA	Hydr.	1000	(Turbine)	73'-9"	59'-3"	11/67-11/68	4[1]	10[1]	None
Frangeco	Hydr.	1140	(Turbine)	86'-1"	55'-8"	7/73-2/75	12	None	None
Rohr	Hydr.[2]	1140	(Turbine)	87'-2.23"	55'-8.5"	7/76-11/76	14	None	None
MLW	A.c.	2700	16	67'-11"	41'-0"	8/73	None	1	None
MLW	A.c.	2700	16	67'-10"	39'-2"	1979-1980[3]	2[3]	22[3]	None
Werkspoor	D.c.	2000	32	79'-6"	52'-1"	5/77-8/77[4]	None	4	None

[1] Two of the 10 Canadian units were subsequently resold in the U.S.

[2] Westinghouse traction motor connected to hydraulic transmission for third-rail operation into Grand Central Terminal, New York.

[3] As of this writing, these were units on order for Amtrak and VIA Rail Canada.

[4] Secondhand delivery dates to Ontario Northland Railway after *Trans Europe Express* service; built 1960.

The first of the recent lightweight train attempts was the United Aircraft Turbotrain of 1967. Two train sets (four power units) were built by Pullman-Standard for United Aircraft for sale to the Department of Transportation. After tests, they began service on Penn Central's ex-New Haven line between New York and Boston in April 1969. After the creation of Amtrak, these trains continued in that service until retired in September 1975 because of poor mechanical reliability (60 per cent availability). As of this writing they were stored at Ivy City engine terminal, Washington, D.C., pending sale. At the same time as the two DOT sets were built (road Nos. 50-53), five sets (10 power units) were assembled in Canada by MLW for United Aircraft for delivery to Canadian National. CN intended to use these trains to replace Montreal-Toronto conventional-train *Rapido* service, but mechanical problems vexed these sets also. Not until 1973 was CN able to establish a reliable service, using three of the original five pairs of power units. The other two pairs were sold to Amtrak in 1973, but one pair was destroyed in a collision before delivery could be accomplished; the surviving set sold to Amtrak was retired in

Continued

1975 along with the Pullman-built sets and sent to Ivy City to hold for sale. The three CN pairs were conveyed to VIA Rail Canada. On CN they were numbered 125/150, 126/151, and 129/154. The set destroyed was to have been Amtrak 54/55, and the set sold to Amtrak became 56/57.

Despite the difficult experience with the UA turbos, Amtrak was determined to experiment with two leased turbine train sets produced by ANF-Frangeco of France (four power units, Amtrak 60/61 and 62/63). When these "Turboliners" proved moderately successful in service out of Chicago, four more train sets (eight power units) were ordered, Amtrak 58/59, 64/65, 66/67, 68/69, bringing the total to six train sets. At the same time, to avoid being criticized for making non-American purchases, Amtrak arranged to purchase additional Turboliners to be built under license by Rohr Industries—7 sets (14 power units) numbered 150-163. These sets were based at Rensselaer, N.Y., and used in the New York-Niagara Falls corridor. Rohr went out of the rail car business after delivery of these trains, and both the Rohr and Frangeco trains experienced high operating costs compared to diesel-powered Amfleet trains, so it is not likely the Amtrak turbine experiment will go any further.

In the meantime, MLW introduced a turbine-competitive diesel model, the M429LRC (for "Light, Rapid, Comfortable") with leveling devices on the locomotive and MLW-built cars to permit higher curve speeds. The demonstrator toured the U.S.A. and Canada, making several tests.

Ontario Northland bypassed the home-built product in favor of secondhand *Trans Europe Express* equipment.

UA Turbotrain

These photos offer a comparison of the Canadian- and U.S.-assembled UA turbotrain power cars. The U.S. version hauled only one trailer between the two power units; the Canadian version originally hauled five trailers between the power units, increased to seven in 1972. The extra cars came from the two sets sold to Amtrak (one of which was destroyed before delivery), so that the ex-CN set on Amtrak had only two trailers between the power units instead of the original five. Wheel arrangement of the power cars is B-1.

Jack Armstrong.

Larry Russell.

ANF-Frangeco Turboliner

Louis A. Marre.

Rohr Turboliner

The French-built turboliner can be easily distinguished from the U.S.-built licensee version by Rohr by the turret cab nose of the French version compared to the continuous curve from pilot beam to roof on the Rohr's. Wheel arrangement of both versions is B-2.

Marre-Mott collection, Jack Armstrong.

LRC demonstrator

The knife prow of the LRC with its square headlights is not likely to be confused with anything else. Wheel arrangement of the power car is B-B.

Marre-Mott collection, Gordon B. Mott.

Werkspoor-Utrecht push-pull train

The distinctive Dutch rounded nose and windshield pattern (also found on the Dutch railways' M.U. electric trains) identifies these exiles on Ontario Northland. There is only one power car per train, with a cab car at the rear for push-pull operation (not used on ON, which prefers to keep the heavy power car in the lead for crossing protection). The B-B power car contains two 16-cylinder diesel engines for traction plus a 300 h.p. auxiliary diesel engine for "hotel" power for train heating and lighting.

TRAINS: J. David Ingles.

ELECTRIC LOCOMOTIVES PRESENTLY IN USE

Electrification has declined in North America rather than advanced as overseas, so the opportunities for spotting electric locomotives are fairly limited. For purposes of comprehensiveness, though, it is desirable to include in this guide the types of mainline electric locomotives operating on our continent. In this chapter a.c./a.c. or a.c./d.c. refers to transmission current and traction motor current. A.c./a.c. means a.c. transmission to the locomotive and a.c. traction motors. A.c./d.c. means that some form of rectification is used to derive d.c. motor current out of a.c. current transmitted to the pantograph. The heading "c.h.p." refers to the continuous horsepower rating of the locomotive, which can be exceeded on a short-time basis for acceleration. Traction current is given instead of cylinders, and is expressed in terms of volts and cycles at the pantograph—11kv. 25hz. means 11,000 volts, 25 hertz.

DUAL-SERVICE CARBODY ELECTRIC LOCOMOTIVE, 4800 C.H.P. 2-C + C-2

Type	Builder	A.c./d.c.	H.p.	Current	Length	Truck centers	Period produced	Approx. No. of units sold		
								U.S.A.	Canada	Mexico
GG1	GE, PRR	A.c./a.c.	4800	11kv. 25hz.	79"-6"	Articulated	9/34-6/43	139	None	None

Threatened with retirement because of the Northeast Corridor Project voltage and cycle change, the GG1 is otherwise still a sound operating entity, as demonstrated by its ability, in 1978-79, to handle *Metroliner* schedules with single locomotives. Locomotives 4800-4814 were built by GE at Erie, Pa.; the remainder were built at Altoona, Pa., using electrical equipment furnished by GE and Westinghouse.

GG1

Conrail 4800 is the original GG1, with riveted carbody. All subsequent GG1's have a welded skin, as found on Amtrak's "Pennsylvania" 4935 (facing page)—a recreation of the original GG1 paint scheme, which Amtrak graciously permitted in 1977.

Marre-Mott collection, Herbert H. Harwood Jr.

GG1

PASSENGER-SERVICE CARBODY ELECTRIC LOCOMOTIVE, 4000 C.H.P. C-C

Type	Builder	A.c./d.c.	H.p.	Current	Length	Truck centers	Period produced	Approx. No. of units sold		
								U.S.A.	Canada	Mexico
EP-5	GE	A.c./d.c.	4000	11kv. 25hz.[1]	68'-0"	44'-0"	3/55-6/55	10	None	None

Supplemental ability to work off 600v. d.c. third rail for operation in and out of Grand Central Terminal, N.Y.

As of 1979 the surviving six units of this group were stored at Harrisburg, Pa., but were being considered by Northeast Corridor personnel for conversion to 26kv. 60hz. to release a like number of Amtrak E60CP's to Conrail for freight service in place of retired freight GG1's. The EP-5's are former New Haven Railroad passenger locomotives and were the first production ignitron rectifier locomotives in the United States.

EP-5

Marre-Mott collection, Ken Douglas.

HIGH HORSEPOWER ELECTRIC ROAD-SWITCHERS, 2500 C.H.P. B-B; 3300, 5000, 6000 C.H.P. C-C; 10,000 C.H.P. B-B-B

Type	Builder	A.c./d.c.	H.p.	Current	Length	Truck centers	Period produced	Approx. No. of units sold		
								U.S.A.	Canada	Mexico
E25B	GE	A.c./d.c.	2500	25kv. 60hz.	61'-2"	37'-10"	5/76-date	7+	None	None
E33	GE	A.c./d.c.	3300	11kv. 25hz.	69'-6"	45'-0"	10/56-2/57	12	None	None
E44	GE	A.c./d.c.	5000	11kv. 25hz.	69'-6"	45'-0"	12/60-7/63	66	None	None
E50C	GE	A.c./d.c.	5000	25kv. 60hz.	69'-6"	45'-0"	5/68	2	None	None
GM6	EMD	A.c./d.c.	6000	11kv. 25hz.	68'-10"	43'-6"	4/75	1	None	None
GM10	EMD	A.c./d.c.	10000	11kv. 25hz.	76'-4"	22'-0"/22'-0"	7/76	1	None	None

The E25B, developed for Texas Utilities, Inc., falls out of a chronology that otherwise develops a steady upward rise in rated continuous horsepower. The E25B should actually be classed as a heavy industrial locomotive.

In terms of technological development, the locomotives here called "E33" (their Conrail class) were the first rectifier freight locomotives and the first large electrics in a road-switcher configuration. GE built them for the Virginian Railway. When Virginian merged into Norfolk & Western in 1959, the N&W soon set up traffic flows that made the electrified ex-VGN route a one-way railroad, an uneconomical situation that resulted in discontinuance of the electrification in 1962. The locomotives were then tested on the Pennsylvania,

Continued

E25B

Charles K. Marsh.

but they disrupted PRR's inductive trainphone system because they lacked smoothing reactors. The trainphone system was discontinued in favor of radio the following year, but by that time 11 of the units had been sold to the New Haven. When New Haven was absorbed into PC, the ex-VGN motors began running on former PRR lines, where they remained into Conrail takeover.

The Pennsylvania Railroad in the late 1950's sought replacements for their P5a electrics in freight service. They adopted an uprated version of the Virginian locomotive offered by GE, the E44. Originally rated at 4400 c.h.p., the E44's were rerated to 5000 c.h.p. when equipped with solid-state rectifiers, although they still carry a class of E44 (actually, E44A since uprating).

The latest phase in the development of GE electric road-switchers was the near-duplicate of the E44 furnished to the Muskingum Electric Railroad, the E50C, which was intended by the American Electric Power Co. to be a test tube for commercial frequency distribution without phase balancing.

As railroads began to talk seriously about electrification in the mid-1970's, EMD decided to protect their flank by entering a licensing agreement with the Swedish firm ASEA and built two demonstrators to undergo testing on ex-PRR electrified lines. The GM6 and GM10 were the result.

Both photos, Marre-Mott collection, Herbert H. Harwood Jr.

Conrail 4605 shows its kinship to the E44 by close comparison to Conrail 4456. The wind fairing above the short hood sheltering the pantograph area, and the use of twin Faively pantographs rather than a single traditional type, are the principal differences in appearance. Also, the E33 has a hood-top deck at the rear that formerly carried the bus connectors used to power two locomotives from one pantograph, a feature since removed.

↑ E44

↖ E33

E50C

Comparison of Muskingum 100 with Conrail 4456 on the facing page shows that the locomotives are practically identical. The larger pantograph insulators are a clue to the E50C's higher transmission voltage collection requirement; also, only one pantograph is provided where there is space for two. The Muskingum locomotives operate crewless, though equipped with conventional cabs.

Marre-Mott collection, Don Dover.

GM6

GM10

The GM6 rides an SD40-2 frame, while the GM10, because of its unique trucks and truck arrangement, is on a custom underframe.

HIGH-HORSEPOWER ELECTRIC BOX-CAB LOCOMOTIVES, 5100, 6000 C.H.P. C-C

Type	Builder	A.c./d.c.	H.p.	Current	Length	Truck centers	Period produced	Approx. No. of units sold		
								U.S.A.	Canada	Mexico
E60C	GE	A.c./d.c.	5100	50kv. 60hz.	63'-2"	36'-10"	12/72-10/76	6	None	None
E60CP	GE	A.c./d.c.	6000	11kv. 25hz.	71'-3"	45'-4"	10/74- /75	7	None	None
E60CH	GE	A.c./d.c.	6000	11kv. 25hz.	71'-3"	45'-4"	/75-8/75	19	None	None

The evolution back to box-cabs in more-recent orders for high-horsepower electrics may be more accidental than purposeful. In the blowing sands of Arizona on the Black Mesa & Lake Powell, for which the E60C's were designed, the sealed box-cab has obvious advantages. On the other hand, the E60CP and CH models for Amtrak were not designed as road-switchers for reasons of appearance. Because of the tracking problems which held up delivery of the Amtrak units during 1975 (and which coincided with similar problems with the SDP40F diesels), Amtrak became disenchanted with the locomotives—FRA limited them to 90 mph in a corridor where Amtrak wants to operate at 110 mph and up. Hence, it appears these units will eventually be sold to Conrail to replace freight GG1's, and the new ASEA-EMD B-B's will replace E60's in corridor passenger service.

E60C

The Black Mesa & Lake Powell box-cabs are distinguished from the later, passenger E60C's by having a cab at just one end.

Marre-Mott collection, Kenneth M. Ardinger.

E60CP

Marre-Mott collection, Gordon B. Mott.

E60CH

The E60CP is distinguished from the E60CH only by the steam generator roof appurtenances visible just behind the cab roof opposite the pantograph end. An E60CH, such as Amtrak 968, has just a roof vent for the head-end power alternator at this position.

Marre-Mott collection, Herbert H. Harwood Jr.

HIGH HORSEPOWER ELECTRIC BOX-CAB LOCOMOTIVES, B-B

Type	Builder	A.c./d.c.	H.p.	Current	Length	Truck centers	Period produced	Approx. No. of units sold		
								U.S.A.	Canada	Mexico
AEM7	EMD			11kv. 25hz.				Under construction at press time		

Under construction at press time were 8 ASEA licensed locomotives patterned on demonstrator X-995, lent by the Swedish State Railways and operated by Amtrak between New York and Washington during 1976-77. The X-995 was returned to Sweden in 1977 but the photograph below may forecast the general appearance of the EMD copies.

AEM7

Donna Marvel.

97

MONTREAL SUBURBAN SERVICE ELECTRIC LOCOMOTIVES

Type	Builder	A.c./d.c.	H.p.	Current	Length	Truck centers	Period produced	Approx. No. of units sold		
								U.S.A.	Canada	Mexico
Box-cab	GE	D.c./d.c.	1100	2400v.	37'-4"	Articulated	6/14-11/16	None	6	None
Center-cab	GE	D.c./d.c.	1100	2400v.	42'-9.9"	21'-0"	7/50	None	3	None
Box-cab	EE[1]	D.c./d.c.	1100	2400v.	40'-0"	Articulated	/24- /26	None	9	None

[1] English Electric

The type designations here have no official status, but are handy for purposes of this book. The GE box-cabs are the original equipment of the Mount Royal Tunnel electrification. The GE center-cab locomotives strongly resemble center-cab diesels and were purchased to supplement the box-cab fleet as traffic grew. The English Electric box-cabs were bought from the Montreal Harbours Board during World War II to increase the capacity of the commuter line.

GE box-cab

The three photos on these pages represent the GE box-cab, GE center-cab and English Electric box-cab locomotives of the Mount Royal Tunnel electrification.

TRAINS: J. David Ingles.

Both photos, Larry Russell collection, J. Pattenaude.

GE center-cab

English Electric

IRON ORE COMPANY OF CANADA ELECTRIC LOCOMOTIVES, 1200 C.H.P. B-B

Type	Builder	A.c./d.c.	H.p.	Current	Length	Truck centers	Period produced	Approx. No. of units sold		
								U.S.A.	Canada	Mexico
SW1200MG	GMD	A.c./d.c.	1200	2300v. 60hz.	44'-6"	22'-0"	1963-1971	None	9	None

General Motors Diesel, Ltd. of London, Ont., produced for Iron Ore Company of Canada these motor-generator locomotives for fully automatic operation at Labrador City, Labr. Not only was the SW1200MG GM's first electric locomotive, it was ostensibly built on an ordinary SW1200 frame. This illustrated the principle of simply "pulling out the engine and dropping in a rectifier bank" which some have suggested for electric locomotive construction; however, these locomotives narrowly preceded the universal acceptance of solid state rectification and used the older motor-generator concept instead. Although the SW1200MG's rode on Blomberg trucks, they did not turn out to be exactly like all-electric SW1200's, but they were close.

SW1200MG

Peter Cox collection, courtesy Larry Russell.

CAPITAL REBUILD PROGRAM RAILROAD SHOPS

A Capital Rebuild Program (CRP) is an accounting device that allows railroads to treat rebuilt locomotives as if they were new investments. To qualify as a CRP under ICC and IRS rules, the rebuilding costs must exceed half the original purchase price of the locomotive. The railroad can then depreciate the rebuilt locomotive over its entire anticipated additional life (usually 8 to 10 or even 15 years). Otherwise, the rebuilding expenses must be treated as maintenance costs in the year the repairs were made and there are no tax advantages.

In addition, a CRP qualifies for an investment tax credit. However, because most railroads use up their allowable investment credits on other projects, they often sell the rebuilt locomotive to a lessor who then leases the locomotive to the railroad at a lower cost than the railroad would have to pay to borrow cash for repairs. Such leases are profitable to both parties because the lessor receives an investment tax credit and shares the benefit with the railroad through a lower interest rate on the lease. These "leverage leases" theoretically allow the railroad to take title to the locomotive at the end of the leasing period, but in most cases the railroad surrenders the locomotive to the lessor because of the high "buy-out" price, and because major overhaul expenses often coincide with the expiration of the lease. The frequency with which railroads choose to buy out at the end of these leases versus surrendering the locomotive depends on the condition of the locomotive at the end of the lease and the extent to which inflation has diminished the buy-out price in real dollars.

An almost-standard package of work has developed for capital rebuilding of locomotives. The candidates are almost always GP7, GP9, SD7, or SD9 locomotives because few GE locomotives are old enough to qualify for rebuild and because other non-EMD makes, being out of production, are poor long-term prospects for parts availability, even if their maintenance cost history justified rebuilding. On a typical large railroad there are many possibilities

for low-mileage operations where a GP7/9 or SD7/9 is ideal, and capital rebuilding offers an intermediate economic choice between continued maintenance overhauls of such power and replacement with new. EMD's GP15-1 is a direct response to the competition of such rebuildings against new power purchases.

The standard package which characterizes such rebuildings often includes upgrading to use "E" power assemblies (that is, 645 engine dimensions), but this cannot be done to "B" engine heads without almost-prohibitive reworking of the decks. So, if a GP7 or SD7 is the candidate, the railroad may have to swap around to find a C engine on which the E heads will fit, or settle for a less-satisfactory "BC" conversion which retains the old B head and uses a water jumper to get around the B engine water leak problems. In either case, a minor increase in horsepower often results, because even with 567-dimension BC engines the package usually includes the four-stack "liberated exhaust" system pioneered by Missouri Pacific, which enables the higher horsepower rating.

The standard package also usually includes complete rewiring to eliminate deteriorated insulation, although in most cases the electrical system is rebuilt using the old-style large contactors instead of the more recent modular electronics.

Generally, the air brakes on a CRP engine are upgraded to contemporary 26L, although sometimes a minimum 6BLC-type conversion is made to allow M.U. with other 26L or 24RL power. Also, such peripheral changes as chop noses, retention toilets, FRA-mandated footboard removal and related pin-lifter modifications are accomplished. The usual reconditioning of such components as radiators, air compressor, and fuel and water pumps, which would be done in any heavy overhaul, is also performed.

Most CRP locomotives have been converted to central engine air filtration systems, using the prominent hood-top air intake and filter assembly.

Continued

The future of CRP programs depends on several things. Most important is the question of amount and quality of repair parts. EMD naturally gives first preference to new locomotives for its parts production. There is a fixed pool of older parts that can be reconditioned, and some of those are getting beyond the point of economical reconditioning. Some reconditioned parts furnished by other vendors have been of poor quality. There are also the questions of whether the railroad's shop forces can perform the work competitively with the GP15-1 alternative, and whether the cost is competitive with simple heavy overhaul.

EMD SWITCHERS, REBUILT BY RAILROAD, 1000-1300 H.P. B-B

Railroad/model[1]	Engine	H.p.	Cyls.	Length	Truck centers	Period produced	Approx. No. produced	Railroad shop location
IC/ICG SW1300	567BC	1300	12	44'-5"	22'-0"	10/71-date	21 +[2]	Paducah, Ky.
IC SW1	645E	1000	8	44'-5"	22'-0"	10/68	1	Paducah, Ky.
BN NW12	645E	1200	12	44'-5"	22'-0"	2/75-10/76	4	W. Burlington, Ia.
C&NW NW2	567B	1000	12	44'-5"	22'-0"	5/73-?	8 +	Oelwein, Ia.
AT&SF SSB1200	567BC	1200	12	44'-5"	22'-0"	1/75-	6 +	San Bernardino, Calif.

[1] These are unofficial model designations applied by the railroad, except where the SW1 or NW2 designation was retained.
[2] Includes three calves.

Paul C. Hunnell.

Kenneth M. Ardinger.

J. David Ingles.

ICG's program began under Illinois Central auspices in 1967 with the rebuilding of SW7 No. 1200 to No. 200, with no increase in the original (1200) horsepower. In the same year, IC purchased Louisiana Midland SW7 No. 10 and rebuilt it to No. 236; also, IC SW7 425 and SW9 479 were rebuilt to 325 and 379. In 1969 seven SW7's and SW9's were rebuilt as 1244-1250, a number series which placed them on top of the then-existing 1200 class, again with no horsepower increase. All the foregoing have been treated as maintenance overhauls and thus not included in the table. However, in 1968 one SW1, No. 612, was substantially upgraded and renumbered to 13, as illustrated on the facing page. Then, between October 1971 and October 1973 cow-calf sets 1300-1300B to 1302-1302B were converted from TR2's and switchers 1303-1305, and afterwards all carried the "SW1300" railroad designation. The switcher program was then discontinued until 1978 when four locomotives in the new 1400 series were produced, noted for their angled cab roofs.

Kenneth M. Ardinger collection, W. S. Kuba.

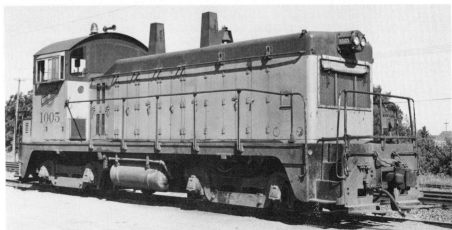

Marre-Mott collection, Louis A. Marre.

BN began an ambitious program to heavily rework old NW2's, but completed only four before deciding that the program was not economic. A front number board/headlight structure similar to that found on SW1000/SW1001/SW1500's identifies these units, as well as their low road numbers: 1, 5, 14, and 19.

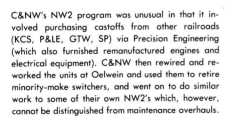

C&NW's NW2 program was unusual in that it involved purchasing castoffs from other railroads (KCS, P&LE, GTW, SP) via Precision Engineering (which also furnished remanufactured engines and electrical equipment). C&NW then rewired and reworked the units at Oelwein and used them to retire minority-make switchers, and went on to do similar work to some of their own NW2's which, however, cannot be distinguished from maintenance overhauls.

W. S. Kuba.

AT&SF's SSB1200 program (for "Switcher, San Bernardino, 1200 h.p.") has thus far involved NW2's and SW9's, with 1239 an example of the latter.

EMD ROAD-SWITCHERS, REBUILT BY RAILROAD, 1500-2000 H.P. B-B

Railroad/model[1]	Engine	H.p.	Cyls.	Length	Truck centers	Period produced	Approx. No. produced	Railroad shop location
MILW "GP20"[2]	645E	2000	16	56'-2"	31'-0"	6/69-2/70	18	Milwaukee, Wis.
MILW "GP20"[3]	645E	2000	16	56'-2"	31'-0"	4/72-10/73	36	Milwaukee, Wis.
IC/ICG GP8	567BC	1600	16	55'-11"[4]	31'-0"	9/67-date	123[6]	Paducah, Ky.
IC/ICG GP10	567C	1850	16	56'-2"[4]	31'-0"	6/67-date	343[6]	Paducah, Ky.
ICG GP11[5]	567C	1850	16	55'-11"	31'-0"	4/78-date	1[6]	Paducah, Ky.
SP GP9E	567C	1750	16	56'-2"	31'-0"	2/70-date	236 + [7]	Sacramento, Calif.[8]
BN GP10	645E	1800	16	55'-11"	31'-0"	7/74-11/76	26	W. Burlington, Ia.
AT&SF CF7	567BC	1500	16	55'-11"	31'-0"	2/70-3/78	233	Cleburne, Tex.
AT&SF GP7	567BC	1500	16	55'-11"	31'-0"	11/72-date	140 +	Cleburne, Tex.
AT&SF GP9	567C	1750	16	56'-2"	31'-0"	1/78-date	18 +	Cleburne, Tex.
C&NW GP7	567B, BC	1500	16	55'-11"[4]	31'-0"	/72-date	?	Oelwein, Ia.
C&NW GP9	567C, D	1750	16	56'-2"[4]	31'-0"	10/72-date	20 +	Oelwein, Ia.
CR GP7, GP9	567B, C	1500, 1750	16	55'-11", 56'-2"	31'-0"	1977-78	25	Altoona, Pa.

[1] These are unofficial model designations applied by the railroad, except where the original GP7 or GP9 designation has been retained.

[2] This group did not originally have central air filtration (later this feature was being retrofitted). Rebuilt from GP9's.

[3] This group rebuilt from GP9's and equipped with central air filtration.

[4] Length assumes use of GP7 frame for GP8, and GP9 frame for GP10. Due to exchange of frames in rebuilding and use of C engines in rebuilding GP7's to GP10's, this assumption often does not hold true. The same is true of GP7 and GP9 rebuilds on Chicago & North Western.

[5] Improved version of the GP10 with a single central blower for generator and traction motors, and Dash 2-style modular electronics. Cab moved forward one foot on the frame.

[6] Production through 1978, for IC/ICG only; that is, not including identical units done under contract for other railroads—see following chapter.

[7] Production through 1977; potential is 311 units if all remaining SP GP9's are rebuilt.

[8] Except 14 units done at Houston, Tex.

Missouri Pacific is not listed in the table of capital rebuilds of 1500-2000 h.p. B-B EMD road-switchers because the extensive modification of their fleet has been done as maintenance instead of as a specified capital rebuild program. Nonetheless the results are similar. The North Little Rock shop is geared for extensive component remanufacture, making upgrading routine. The four-stack liberated exhaust manifold, pioneered by MP (and illustrated here on GP18 1930) became a standard feature of CRP modifications on other roads. Lately, as on 1930, MP has also used the central air intake/air-filter box which projects upward behind the forward fan (this is a rear view of the unit). This has been a common item in CRP programs. With its use, all engine air is ingested through the filter box, instead of through the hood louvers, which, however, continue to furnish air for the traction-motor blowers and generator cooling. On other roads, this box is often fitted with weather hoods projecting around the sides of the hood, giving rise to the "ox-yoke" appearance, as it is sometimes called. MP rebuilds often are uprated; for example, 1600 h.p. GP7's.

Louis A. Marre.

The Illinois Central's Paducah shops program was a pioneer CRP, although it owed something to emulation of Missouri Pacific. GP10 8109 was the first GP10 and 7960 was the first GP8; both are illustrated on this page. They, along with GP10's 8009, 8025, and 8082 retained their high noses. The first chopped-nose Paducah was 7961 (facing page), outshopped in March 1968, and the Paducah rebuilds had this feature thereafter. During 1968, there was a brief flirtation with raising the rebuilds to 2000 h.p. rating, which was done temporarily to GP8's 7957, 7964, 7966, 7971, 7981, and GP10's 8004, 8025, 8072, 8158, and 8233. In addition, GP10 8082, rated at 1750 h.p. when rebuilt in December 1967, was rerated to 2000 h.p. in September 1968. Eventually all the 2000 h.p. units were derated to 1850 h.p. The five 7900's mentioned are included in the table as GP8's but considering their horsepower rating, they should now be counted among the GP10's. Since exchanges of C and B engines will probably occur frequently in normal maintenance, other such crossovers will probably occur in the Paducah ranks. The 2000 h.p. period lasted from June 1968 to February 1969. GP10 8031 in March 1969 resumed normal 1850 h.p. production of that type, while GP8 7968 resumed normal 1600 h.p. production of that type in April. The 7968 (illustrated) was also equipped with paper air filters, with the characteristic hood-top box, as were subsequent GP8's and GP10's. All the uprated units have the four-stack liberated exhaust manifold.

IC was pleased with the performance of its rebuilds, and decided that Paducah shops should go into the business of upgrading for others as well. So, a joint venture was started with Precision National Corp. (PNC) of Mount Vernon, Ill., in which IC did the work for Precision under contract (see the following chapter). At the same time, IC began to work through Precision to obtain secondhand GP7's and GP9's to rebuild and add to its own roster. Of the GP8's in the table, 59 are based on secondhand units acquired by IC/ICG. Of the GP10's, 60 are secondhand. Attributing particular GP8's and GP10's to particular original locomotives can be misleading. When a group of units is on the floor at once, there is free mixing of components, so the official identification of a

Continued on page 109

J. David Ingles.

Kenneth M. Ardinger collection, James B. Holder.

108

certain unit as the predecessor of a given GP8 or GP10 (or GP11) is a matter of accounting. For example, ICG 8270, a GP10 outshopped in December 1971., was built on the frame of wrecked B&M GP9 1710 purchased from Precision, but incorporated components from wrecked SP GP9 No. 3516. The 3516 was made the official predecessor while B&M 1710 was charged against 8016, outshopped March 1977.

The IC-GM&O merger had no effect on the CRP program since GM&O had no GP7's or GP9's. ICG briefly considered using the ex-GM&O shop at Iselin, Tenn., as a second CRP facility because of conflict between contract work and ICG's own program. The idea was never carried out, and therefore there have been long gaps in the ICG program because contracts have preempted Paducah's floor space with GP8's and GP10's for Conrail, Alaska, N&W, etc. along with wreck rebuilds or overhauls for foreign-line roads.

On units built for its own use, ICG removes the dynamic braking and eliminates the characteristic blister. None of the IC's own GP7's or GP9's were so equipped, but many of the secondhand units have been.

W. S. Kuba.

J. David Ingles collection, J. W. Stubblefield.

There is little difference between the C and D engines, so a GP10 can be based on a GP18 as well as a GP9. ICG 8418, outshopped in July 1974, illustrates this. The 8418 was rebuilt from a wrecked GTW GP18, but because of wreck damage, the lineage was not so evident. The numbering system used with the Paducah rebuilds is hard to summarize, because the system changed in midstream. Originally, the numbers of all rebuilds were lowered by 1000 from their original IC numbers; e.g., 7960 was the former 8960. The 7700 series was opened up for foreign-road GP7's being rebuilt into GP8's, while the series 8267-8299 was opened for this purpose for GP10's, as were 8390-8399 and 8429-8499. The slots 7982-7999 were for GP8's. For the most part, numbering followed this pattern until 1977, when ICG began to fill vacant spots in the number blocks with locomotives regardless of former number or owner, apparently in an effort to make solid blocks of numbers that would be easier to deal with in documents. At this writing, the following number blocks existed:

7700-7736 GP8	7981 GP8	8199 GP10	8279-8283 GP10	8370, 8371 GP10
7737 GP8	7983-7999 GP8	8202-8205 GP10	8285-8296 GP10	8375 GP10
7738-7746 GP8	8000 GP10	8207 GP10	8301-8306 GP10	8377 GP10
7764 GP8	8002-8075 GP10	8209-8215 GP10	8308-8332 GP10	8379 GP10
7800 GP8	8077-8093 GP10	8217 GP10	8335 GP10	8383 GP10
7850-7852 GP8	8095-8128 GP10	8219-8230 GP10	8337 GP10	8387 GP10
7900-7918 GP8	8130-8144 GP10	8233-8237 GP10	8339 GP10	8390-8397 GP10
(7900 ex-7982)	8146-8148 GP10	8240 GP10	8343 GP10	8418 GP10
7950 GP8	8150-8171 GP10	8243 GP10	8346-8348 GP10	8442-8447 GP10
7952-7955 GP8	8173-8181 GP10	8245 GP10	8351 GP10	8460-8463 GP10
7957 (rerated to GP10	8183, 8184 GP10	8247-8251 GP10	8354 GP10	8465, 8466 GP10
7960-7972 GP8 (7964, 7966, 7971 rerated to GP10)	8186-8197 GP10	8254 GP10	8357-8359 GP10	
7974 GP8		8256-8260 GP10	8361, 8362 GP10	
7976 GP8		8265-8276 GP10	8365 GP10	
7978, 7979 GP8				

Marre-Mott collection, Lee Hastman.

On its own GP8's and GP10's, ICG originally favored a Pyle Gyralite oscillating headlight, mounted between the number indicators over the windshield. Finding that the rotating mechanism of this light caused maintenance difficulties, ICG converted to a solid-state alternating-light fixture having three lights arranged one above the other in the old Gyralite location. The top two white lights alternate with each other, one aimed down and to the right, one aimed down and to the left, simulating the old Gyralite sweep. The third, bottom light is red, and comes on automatically at an emergency brake application, stopping trains which might be passing on double track. The last Gyralite unit was 8307, and the first solid-state-light unit was 8444, both outshopped in January 1974.

The latest variation in the Paducah rebuilds is the group having angled cab roofs similar to contemporary EMD factory power. This is primarily due to the making of new cabs from scratch for 25 UP GP9B's starting with 8462, outshopped in June 1977. However, GP8 7800, outshopped in July 1977, also has such a cab, although nominally based on a P&LE GP7. Railroads whose GP7's, GP9's, or GP18's have become the basis of ICG GP8's or GP10's include DT&I, P&LE, RDG, SLSF, QNS&L, C&O, B&O, B&M, D&RGW, CRR, FEC, and UP. The influx of foreign units is providing ICG with sufficient power to retire the Alco power it inherited from GM&O, as well as to handle traffic growth.

TRAINS: J. David Ingles.

Starting in March 1977, ICG rebuilds incorporated a more compact form of central air filter, the single-stage Dynacell, as shown on ICG 8016, the first unit so equipped.

W. S. Kuba.

ICG 8301 built in 1978 is the prototype GP11. The provision of the Dash 2 electrical cabinet requires complete reworking of the cab. The installation of a central equipment blower also requires relocation of the cab one foot forward as compared to GP7/9 layout. The equipment blower is evident in left-side views through the ducts on the hood side just behind the cab; the ducts then run back on top of the left-side running board to service the rear traction motors.

Courtesy Illinois Central Gulf Railroad.

MILW 999 was the first in that railroad's program, under which rebuilds were numbered downward from 999. Externally, the chopped nose and the affixing of a GP20 model plate was the only evidence of the change. MILW 971 illustrates the second group, which incorporated the paper air-filter package with weather hoods, and also employed a larger number box above the windshield.

SP's GP9E's, having no chopped noses (except for GP9's built that way originally) and no weather hoods on their paper air-filter boxes, are inconspicuous.

BN's GP10's were "Cadillacs," so much so that continuation of the program could not be justified after it was interrupted by the 1975 recession. Two incomplete units were released in 1976, and BN went back to overhauling GP7's in kind, as all capital monies went toward purchasing new SD40-2's and C30-7's for coal service. Hooded paper air-filter boxes and four-stack manifolds make the 1400's easy to spot.

C&NW's GP7 program primarily involved rewiring, and in most cases did not qualify as capital rebuilding although chopping of noses and blanking the dynamic brake blisters on many of the resulting 4300's and 4400's produced a CRP look.

C&NW's GP9 program (4500's) more closely resembled the CRP programs on ICG, with extensive rewiring, reworking of engine components, chopping of noses, and adding of four-stack manifolds. In removing the dynamic braking from its rebuilds, C&NW left the blister on but blanked it off. Not all rebuilds have the brake blisters, though, because CNW's own GP9's didn't have dynamic braking; only M&StL and some foreign-line units purchased for rebuild have the blister. Like ICG, C&NW has purchased other roads' GP7's and GP9's for rebuild to retire minority-make power on its own property. As an added twist, some foreign GP9's came out as 4300's (GP7's) because they were powered with 567B engines from F units sent to Precision for remanufacture.

Marre-Mott collection, W. S. Kuba.

Marre-Mott collection. Jack Armstrong.

Unique among CRP locomotives is the Santa Fe CF7 ("Converted F7") for which it was necessary for the railroad to manufacture new underframes. In the original CRP configuration, as illustrated by 2647, the old F7 roof line was maintained in the reconstructed cab; even the roll-down F-unit side windows with wing windows were kept. The first CF7, 2649, had dynamic braking because the salvaged GP7 employed had it; all the later CF7's, numbered downward from 2649, had homemade hoods like that on 2647, without dynamics.

Both photos, Marre-Mott collection, J. R. Quinn.

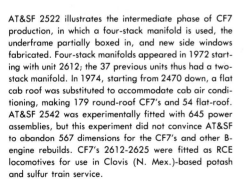

AT&SF 2522 illustrates the intermediate phase of CF7 production, in which a four-stack manifold is used, the underframe partially boxed in, and new side windows fabricated. Four-stack manifolds appeared in 1972 starting with unit 2612; the 37 previous units thus had a two-stack manifold. In 1974, starting from 2470 down, a flat cab roof was substituted to accommodate cab air conditioning, making 179 round-roof CF7's and 54 flat-roof. AT&SF 2542 was experimentally fitted with 645 power assemblies, but this experiment did not convince AT&SF to abandon 567 dimensions for the CF7's and other B-engine rebuilds. CF7's 2612-2625 were fitted as RCE locomotives for use in Clovis (N. Mex.)-based potash and sulfur train service.

Marre-Mott collection, J. R. Quinn.

AT&SF 2064 (conventional cab) and AT&SF 2088 (flat-roof cab) illustrate the GP7 CRP program which began on AT&SF with the outshopping of 2050 (the former 2834) in November 1972. A similar program began in 1978 for GP9's. The CRP locomotives have four-stack manifolds and chopped noses. Note that neither the CF7's nor these locomotives have paper air filters. Locomotives 2050-2067, 2246, and 2247 have the conventional cab roof outline, while 2068-up have the flat cab roof to accommodate cab air conditioning. As with the CF7's, this change began in 1974. The 2246 and 2247 are in a number series covering "mothers" to "drones" (slugs); see last chapter.

118

Marre-Mott collection, James B. Holder.

Louis A. Marre.

Conrail has been relying mainly on contract rebuilds of its GP7/9/18 fleet, but CR 7479 illustrates an Altoona-rebuilt
unit, with new wiring, overhauled engine, paper air filter, blanked dynamic brake blisters, and no chopped nose.

EMD ROAD-SWITCHERS, REBUILT BY RAILROAD, 1500-2600 H.P. C-C

Railroad/model[1]	Engine	H.p.	Cyls.	Length	Truck centers	Period produced	Approx. No. produced	Railroad shop location
UP SD24	645E	3300	16	60'-8"	35'-0"	7/68	1	Omaha, Nebr.
UP SD24-4	567D	2400	16	60'-8"	35'-0"	5/75	1	Omaha, Nebr.
C&NW SD9	567C	1750	16	60'-8"	35'-0"	5/71-	?	Oelwein, la.
MILW SD10	645E	1800	16	60'-8"[2]	35'-0"	3/74-1/76	21	Milwaukee, Wis.
SP SD9E	567C	1750	16	60'-8"	35'-0"	8/70-date	122	Sacramento, Calif.
AT&SF SD26	645E	2650	16	60'-8"	35'-0"	2/73-3/78	80	San Bernardino, Calif.
ICG SD11	645E	2000	16	60'-8"	35'-0"	/79-	20	Paducah, Ky.

[1] These are unofficial model designations by the railroad, except where the original SD9 or SD24 designation has been retained.

[2] Assumes use of SD9 frame; some are from SD7's where this dimension is one half inch longer.

UP 3999, previously numbered 3100, 3200, and 3399 since rebuilding (not to mention its pre-rebuild number of 423) was at one time considered a possible prototype for conversion of UP's entire SD24 fleet. As it turned out, the unit was of more interest as a test bed for the concept of a constant-speed engine (all power variation produced through excitation of the alternator only) and of single-wire electrical systems (no return wires; all circuits using the chassis as ground through appropriate resistances). The constant-speed portion of the experiment was soon concluded, and there were no duplicates, but thereafter the locomotive remained in service as an "almost SD45."

Marre-Mott collection, Keith E. Ardinger

UP 414 was the next attempt at a CRP SD24, using latter-day (but non-modular) electrical components and an AR10 main alternator in place of the original d.c. generator. It, too, failed to become a prototype of a general program, and UP wound up selling most of its SD24's to Precision, where 20 of them became seed for ICG's SD11 program.

Kenneth M. Ardinger collection, George Cockle.

C&NW's program, as befit its approach to the GP7/GP9 rebuilds, was drawn-out and not as extensive as that on some other roads, but new numbers, chopped noses, blanked dynamic brake grids, and a new paint scheme made the rebuilds recognizable.

122

MILW 559 is typical of the SD10's, characterized by chopped noses and hooded paper air-filter intakes. The 559 happens to be on an SD7 frame, as indicated by the solid handrail stanchions.

Southern Pacific 4451 is a 1974 product of their program, and was one of two passenger SD9's to be upgraded (4450, 4451). The Dynacell filter box on the hood top is the only external giveaway to the rebuilding other than renumbering.

Marre-Mott collection, J. R. Quinn.

AT&SF 4600 represents the extensive AT&SF rebuilding of its SD24 fleet. The installation of a central air intake behind the cab displaced the four SD24 rooftop reservoirs to positions farther back along the edge of the hood, making the rebuilds easy to spot.

CAPITAL REBUILDING OF PASSENGER POWER BY RAILROAD

Most U.S. railroads quit the long-haul passenger business with the start-up of Amtrak May 1, 1971, so there have been few occasions for railroads to include passenger power in their capital rebuilding programs. Illinois Central began a passenger rebuild program in 1967, and their E8 fleet was to be included. The program got this far:

E8A rebuilds	E8B rebuilds
4029 renumbered to 2021 (2/69)	4104 renumbered to 2100 (2/68)
4030 renumbered to 2022 (9/67)	
4032 renumbered to 2024 (7/68)	

In keeping with the early concept of the Paducah program, the rebuilding was entirely in kind, without increase in horsepower. The other significant program on passenger power was Chicago & North Western's conversion of ex-Union Pacific E9B's to "Crandall Cab" units at Oelwein shops. The 11 units, C&NW 501-511, were completed January through May 1973. In keeping with the rest of C&NW's program, other work on the E9B's was of an in-kind overhaul nature. The program also included rebuild of conventional ex-UP E9A's. The E9's were used to replace F units in Chicago suburban service. The Crandall Cab was named for its designer, the late M. H. Crandall, C&NW Assistant Superintendent of Motive Power who succumbed to a heart attack while trying to start a suburban train's locomotive during the January 1979 blizzard. Locomotive 502 has since been named in his honor.

Paul C. Hunnell.

Marre-Mott collection, Jack Armstrong.

127

DETURBOCHARGING

A spreading trend among railroads is to remove the expensive turbochargers from 2000-2500 h.p. EMD's now used in secondary service and substitute 645 power assemblies to obtain a 2000 h.p. rating with a Roots-blower-aspirated engine. Deturbocharging is related to capital rebuilding, but is usually not a true CRP in the accounting sense because the locomotives involved are too new.

Penn Central pioneered deturbocharging with conversion of the ex-New York Central GP20's 2100-2112 (now Conrail 2100-2112) in 1969 and 1970. At the same time, paper air filters were added—one of the earliest applications of this now-common aspect of conversion. The resulting unit looks like a GP20 except for its four-stack liberated-exhaust manifold replacing the single, fat turbo stack, and the projecting paper air-filter box on top of the hood. Subsequent deturbochargings included Southern Pacific/Cotton Belt GP20's, GP30's, and GP35's, Missouri Pacific GP35's, and ICG's ex-UP SD24's converted to SD11's, mentioned earlier in this chapter. More such conversions are likely since turbo maintenance is costly.

Louis A. Marre.

Marre-Mott collection, Vic Reyna.

CAPITAL REBUILD PROGRAM, CONTRACTORS

The economics of capital rebuilding were discussed in the introduction to the previous chapter. However, some railroads either do not have the type of shops, or enough floor space beyond that needed for general overhaul, to do such work themselves. Therefore, the practice of contracting out work of this sort has emerged. The Precision National/ICG Paducah team was the first and largest of the contractor endeavors, followed by Morrison-Knudsen of Boise, Idaho. Rock Island has solicited such work for its Silvis shops, despite the fact that it has had to farm out heavy overhauls to Paducah.

Contract capital rebuilding should be distinguished from the several operations in which simple overhauls are given to units by equipment brokers.

Both of the major contract rebuilders — PNC/Paducah and Morrison-Knudsen — as well as Rock Island's Silvis operation, also do such work in addition to their capital rebuilding.

Like the rebuild programs in the railroad's own shops, contractor rebuilding is limited by the availability of reconditionable EMD engines, or some substitute acceptable to the railroads. In addition, contract shops face the obstacle of railroad labor agreements which may prevent the farming out of shop work. Such labor objections can be overcome if the railroad can demonstrate that it would have otherwise traded in a locomotive without shopping it, and that rebuilding in the railroad's own shop was not a realistic alternative.

CONTRACT REBUILDING: PRECISION NATIONAL

The PNC-ICG partnership performs all major contract rebuild work, and Paducah shops does the work. Thus, PNC rebuilds are nearly identical to contemporary Paducah products for ICG (see EMD ROAD-SWITCHERS, REBUILT BY RAILROAD, 1500-2000 H.P. B-B in previous chapter). However, as Conrail 5407 (a GP8) illustrates, there are some differences, such as the retention of the dynamic brake for customers that want it (as Conrail did). The 5407 is one of a group of 9 GP7's rebuilt at Paducah in 1976 along with 16 GP9's rebuilt to GP10's. Note the use of the lower-profile single-stage Dynacell paper air-filter assembly, which had also come into use on ICG's own units by that time. Ashley, Drew & Northern 1810, a GP10 rebuilt (ironically, from an ICG GP9) in 1978, is similar, but has a Paducah cab, perhaps due to wreck damage of the original. For minor reconditioning, Precision still uses its shop at Mount Vernon, Ill. For example, the work for 40 Conrail units in 1979 was divided between 10 GP9's being reconditioned at Mt. Vernon and 30 GP7's and GP9's being rebuilt at Paducah. With the decision by ICG and PNC to convert

to the GP11 rebuilding concept (again, see the chapter referred to earlier in the paragraph), it is expected that many if not all of the future contract rebuildings of GP7/9's by this partnership will be GP11's.

Marre-Mott collection, J. R. Quinn.

The joint venture between ICG and Precision began in May 1971 with the outshopping of GP10 PNC 3403. PNC-ICG also does lesser contract work for other railroads, such as wreck rebuilds and general overhauls, of which AD&N 1810 is an example; 100 GP7/9's for Rock Island in 1976 were the largest example. That order was especially ironic—shortly after, Rock Island went into the contract rebuilding business at Silvis shops themselves, and did similar overhauls on 30 GP7's for Conrail in 1979.

Marre-Mott collection, Tom King.

FP10 is the designation applied informally to 13 ex-GM&O F3's rebuilt at Paducah in 1979 for Boston's Massachusetts Bay Transit Authority (MBTA), in exchange for traded ex-Conrail GP9's which were in turn rebuilt for other Paducah customers such as Detroit's Southeastern Michigan Transportation Authority (SE-MTA). Four of the F3's, 1150-1153, retained steam generators, while the remaining nine were fitted with head-end engine/alternator sets. The units retained their 1500 h.p.-rated B engines.

Mike Schafer.

CONTRACT REBUILDING: MORRISON-KNUDSEN

After several years of maintaining locomotives (primarily Alcos) purchased secondhand for powering rail construction projects (such as the Libby line change for GN-BN in 1969-70), Morrison-Knudsen, of Boise, Idaho, entered the contract rebuilding field in 1973 with a project to modify 21 BN E9A's for the West Suburban Mass Transit District. The 2400 h.p. rating was retained but 645 power assemblies were substituted. A 500kw. Detroit Diesel auxiliary power plant replaced the steam generator and ventilation was supplied. Two extra cooling fans were installed between the stacks and are plainly evident in the photo of BN 9903. In 1978, four E8A's were rebuilt for WSMTD to the same specification, bringing the total of BN-lettered and BN-maintained E-unit rebuilds to 25, all leased to WSMTD. This contract was followed by the overhauls of several Amtrak E units (a task Amtrak spread around to several railroad and contract shops) and then by the 1975 upgrading of Delaware & Hudson's four PA2's to 2400 h.p. with new 16-cylinder 251 engines. There were no external changes.

Another phase of M-K's program was a more or less standard package

Continued on page 134

Marre-Mott collection, J. R. Quinn.

Marre-Mott collection, Jack Armstrong.

133

which M-K developed for converting an RS3 to a 251-engined, chopnose locomotive of 1800-2000 h.p. The first of these was 1800 h.p. Detroit & Mackinac 974 built from ex-Boston & Maine RS3 1512, completed in December 1974. D&M 974 was followed by 975, a 2000 h.p. version rebuilt from B&M RS3 1517 in 1975, and then by Delaware & Hudson 501-508 (ex-D&H RS3's 4115, 4106, 4107, 4113, 4123, 4112, 4119, and 4128 respectively), completed from December 1975 through March 1976 (illustrated by D&H 501). To accommodate the 251 engine, M-K had to raise the hoods on the D&M and D&H RS3's 6 inches and displace the dynamic brake from its original position above the engine to a box at the top of the hood behind the cab. This modification included a single central traction motor and generator blower behind the cab, with a duct running on top of the left-hand running board (visible in the photo; the handrail stanchions are mounted on it). This same arrangement has been used by EMD since the GP30. At the same time, four similar RS3 rebuilds were done by Green Bay & Western (Nos. 305-308) in its own shops, but without the central blower or dynamic brake. The D&M M-K's also lack these features. The hood-raising problem is the reason C&NW 1621 and 1624 (page 450, THE SECOND DIESEL SPOTTER'S GUIDE) got new hoods when repowered at the factory.

Marre-Mott collection, Jack Armstrong.

Despite its early familiarity with Alcos, M-K was not long in finding out that there was little interest in them on the part of railroads now that Alco was out of business, and that the market was restricted to a very few potential customers. Therefore, even while the Alco-rebuildings on page 134 were in progress, M-K took a more significant step with the purchase of Union Pacific U25B's in 1974. Eight of these units were rebuilt for Weyerhauser Company in 1975-76. UP 637 became Weyerhauser 310 in December 1975, repowered with the 16-567BC engine and D12 generator of an ex-B&O F7. The remaining seven units were for Weyerhauser's Oregon, California & Eastern. OC&E 7601-7605 were virtually identical to the 310 (EMD innards with U25B carbody virtually intact), while 7606-7607 were road slugs (see the last chapter).

Kenneth M. Ardinger.

Two ex-UP U25B's received treatment quite different from the OC&E units, as illustrated by 5302 (which, along with twins 5301 and 5303, has been retained by M-K for lease to various railroads). The U25B underframe is barely recognizable, topped off as it is by an M-K home-built cab and hood. The cab is an adaptation of the Canadian Safety/Comfort Cab concept (except note the rolling door in the nose) and the hood features an adaptation of the EMD radiators and radiator fans, plus panel-type power assembly doors.

Louis A. Marre.

Mike Wise.

Another M-K repowering that used EMD components was Manufacturer's Railway 253, ex-S2 208, outshopped in August 1976, with a 12-567BC engine and EMD generator and cooling-system components. The unit was rated at 1200 h.p.

Marre-Mott collection, C. K. Marsh Jr.

C. K. Marsh Jr. collection, C. E. Harris.

EMD repowerings moved M-K closer to the mainstream in its contract activities, but there remained the problem that work was dependent on a source of reconditioned EMD engines and parts. There was already a great demand for secondhand EMD engines and parts for other rebuilding programs, so M-K took a step in a completely new direction in 1978 by rebuilding four Southern Pacific U25B's with Sulzer engines, SP 7030-7033. These locomotives were intended by M-K as prototypes for other Sulzer repowerings and were attracting railroad attention as a means of introducing more competition into the locomotive field. The SP units included other innovations, such as an imported German unitized radiator system. However, the entry costs for gearing up to large Sulzer locomotive production, even on trade-in underframes, may be more than can be met in the face of uncertain railroad reception.

NOTE: M-K uses a unique model number system for its rebuilds: the tractive effort, followed by the number of powered axles, followed by a code for the type of engine used. Thus, the SP Sulzers are model TE70-4S, the M-K 5301-5303 are model TE53-4E, and the 2000 h.p. RS3 upgrades are model TE56-4A.

Although this system is self-explanatory once understood, it may not work when otherwise dissimilar units come to be rebuilt with the same tractive effort and engine. And since it is not being applied to all-new locomotives, we have not adopted it for classifying M-K power in this book.

REPOWERING BY RAILROAD SHOP

Repowering is a form of capital rebuilding, but it is treated separately here because the repowering programs of the 1950's and 1960's (most of which involved using EMD engines primarily in EMD locomotives) were the precursor to the capital rebuild programs which have come to be such a prominent feature of the contemporary railroad scene. The repowering era is documented in SECOND DIESEL SPOTTER'S GUIDE, pages 433-454; here we will illustrate only some prominent examples which have occurred since that book.

The number of repowerings has been radically reduced for several reasons. First, many otherwise-eligible candidates for repowering were instead traded in. Second, there is a shortage of suitable prime movers because it is hard to get new engines from EMD for this purpose. And third, earlier repowerings were not always very successful because down time remained high after rebuilding due to peripheral systems being outdated or worn out as well as occasional shop-force hostility toward "mongrels."

REPOWERING OF ALCO ROAD-SWITCHERS, 1200-2000 H.P. B-B

Railroad/model	Engine	H.p.	Cyls.	Length	Truck centers	Period produced	Approx. No. produced	Railroad shop location
PC/CR RS3	567B	1200	12	56'-6"	30'-0"	1972-date	55	Altoona, Pa., DeWitt (Syracuse), N.Y.
GB&W RS3	251C	2000	12	56'-6"	30'-0"	1975	4	Green Bay, Wis.
L&N RS3	251C	2000	12	56'-6"	30'-0"	1973	1	Louisville, Ky.

First unit in Penn Central's program (continued by Conrail) to place old E-unit engines in RS3's was this one-of-a-kind with the short hood eliminated entirely, ex-PC 5477, later PC/CR 9950. The locomotive was assigned to yard service, so the change was sensible, but none of the subsequent 54 units have been done this way. Note the addition of hood-top latches above the power assemblies. EMD power assemblies must be lifted higher than Alco's to clear the A-frame of the engine during change-out, hence the need to provide a means for hinging back the top of the hood over the engine.

Marre-Mott collection, Don Dover.

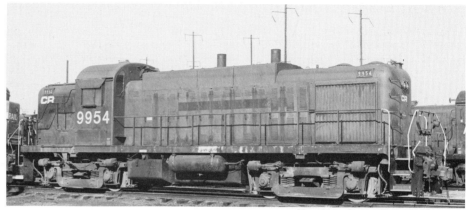

De Witt shops' answer to the power-assembly lift-out problem was to create a boxy structure on top of the hood, allowing the clearance needed without the hinge-and-latch fabrication, as illustrated by 9954.

Conrail 9994 represents the 1978 Altoona program, in which the power-assembly access doors have continued along the pattern set by the noseless 9950. Note the use of twin EMD cooling fans but retention of the Alco radiators. The combined series of Altoona and De Witt repowerings ran 9945-9999 at the end of 1978.

Green Bay & Western and Louisville & Nashville have both done repowerings of RS3's with 251 engines, which requires raising the hood slightly (GB&W's solution) or providing a raised area over the turbocharger (L&N's approach). These repowerings are in addition to contract repowerings of RS3's by Morrison-Knudsen for Delaware & Hudson and Detroit & Mackinac (see previous chapter).

Louis A. Marre.

L&N's sole RS3 repowering is numbered 1350; GB&W's are 305-308.

Louis A. Marre.

REPOWERING OF ALCO ROAD-SWITCHERS, 1200-2050 H.P. C-C

Railroad/model	Engine	H.p.	Cyls.	Length	Truck centers	Period produced	Approx. No. produced	Railroad shop location
PC/CR DL600	567B	1200	12	66'-7"	43'-6"	1/75	1	DeWitt, N.Y.
AT&SF DL600	645E	2050	16	66'-7"	43'-6"	6/74	1	San Bernardino, Calif.

Marre-Mott collection, Thomas M. Trecansky.

Conrail 6849, ex-PC 9949, is permanently paired with an RSD5 slug of the same number. A plan to make a second pair was not carried out. The unit was assigned to De Witt hump yard at Syracuse, N.Y. The unit was PRR/PC 6811/8611 before repowering.

Like Conrail 6849 (previous page), AT&SF 3900, which was to have been a prototype for several similar conversions, became a loner and worked Barstow (Calif.) hump with a slug.

One of the most unusual repowerings—practically a new locomotive (which, incidentally, used the frame of a Baldwin switcher)—is Santa Fe 1160, rebuilt in December 1970 from VO 1000 2220, using a homemade GP7/9-type hood, a 16-567B engine rated at 1500 h.p., an EMD generator, and EMD Blomberg trucks. The locomotive was rebuilt at AT&SF's Cleburne (Tex.) shops and can be regarded as a dress rehearsal for the CF7 program.

NON-POWERED CONVERSIONS OF LOCOMOTIVES

Over the years, a number of locomotive carbodies have been converted to non-powered uses, including cab-control cars and head-end power plants for push-pull commuter trains, steam-generator heater cars, radio remote-control cars, and even fuel tenders.

Primarily, only carbody-type units (usually old F units or similar units of other builders) are suitable for such conversions because they are structurally like passenger cars, and are well suited to accept the same type of equipment put in passenger car bodies. For example, the first heater cars were built to passenger-car specifications (they resembled short baggage cars). But as railroads dieselized and heater-car fleets had to be expanded because freight diesels were often assigned to passenger service, railroads discovered that it was cheaper to convert surplus carbody locomotives than to build additional passenger-carbody heater cars.

Similarly, when head-end lighting systems were developed (as opposed to generators and batteries in each car), they were at first often housed in the baggage portion of a combine. Eventually some railroads decided it was cheaper to house the head-end alternator in a locomotive carbody which could also serve as the control cab for the non-locomotive end of a push-pull train. The Long Island/MTA push-pulls are a prime example.

Northern Pacific's "water baggage cars" provided a precedent of sorts for carbody fuel tenders. NP's locomotive water tank space was limited by boilers, dynamic braking grids, and extra-capacity fuel tanks, so the boiler water supply was trainlined and moved to the baggage car.

It is usually not economical to convert surplus non-carbody locomotives because too much new construction is required and the savings resulting from the use of a ready-made carbody are lost.

HEATER CARS

The first heater cars were built to order in passenger car bodies. Great Northern heater cars 1-4 were an early example, built in 1928 by St. Louis Car Company. They were used on the rear end of passenger trains during extreme cold weather. In the northern tier when a train passes through air chilled to 30 or 40 degrees below zero, even with train speed reduced to 60 mph, heat is transferred out of the cars at a rate which exceeds the ability of the steam line to heat the cars toward the rear of the train. By placing another source of steam at the end of the train and opening the steam line in the middle of the train to exhaust condensate, this problem can be overcome and trains of normal length can be operated instead of running them in sections.

GN cars 1-4 were 43'-8⅛" over their pulling faces, with 26-foot truck centers—comparable in dimensions to an F unit. Cars 1 and 2 became Western Pacific 591 and 592 in 1969, and 3 and 4 lasted to the BN merger. With dieselization, GN built more such cars in the 1940's and up to 1951, mostly using passenger car bodies (express box car bodies were also used, similar to Canadian National's heater cars). Eventually GN replaced the older heater cars with semi-automated cars which would be less labor-intensive to operate (the old cars required a full-time attendant). Ten cars were built: GN/BN 10-19. Car 10 was built in 1965, and cars 11-19 followed in 1966-1967. The cars include indicator lights which inform the head-end crew if the boilers are

Continued

running or have shut down. The cars are automated to the extent of cycling from one boiler to the other at specified intervals unless one boiler goes down, in which case the other remains on. The boilers also blow down automatically. There are two 4500-lb.-per-hour steam generators, 12,000 gallons of boiler water and 1200 gallons of fuel oil capacity on each car, and two GM 220v. diesel generator sets per car to run pumps. The cars have M.U. capability and can be run with the locomotive consist, but were designed to be used at the rear of the train. At Amtrak start-up, BN retained cars 16-19 (though Amtrak often rents them) to protect business car moves and the cars 10-15 went to Amtrak and were renumbered 1910-1915.

Kenneth M. Ardinger.

As Amtrak began running F40PH's, with their electric-only heating capabilities, on trains which still had steam-heated cars, they faced a need for more heater cars. In 1975, six more cars were converted from ex-UP E9B's at ICG's Paducah shops as 1916-1921, later renumbered 666-671. The photo of Amtrak 668 illustrates this conversion. Finally, in 1977 five E8A's were converted to similar cars at Amtrak's Hialeah shop at Miami, Fla., becoming 1922-1926 (672-676; the 675 is illustrated). At the time of this writing, conversion of Amtrak's passenger car fleet to electric heating was proceeding at a pace which would probably preclude the need for making more heater cars.

FUEL TENDER

The use of F40PH's in transcontinental passenger service, with their small fuel tanks, has led to the problem of excess fuel stops—undesirable from a schedule standpoint. In addition, if Amtrak can avoid use of all but a minimum of fueling facilities, it can reduce its payments to contracting railroads for the maintenance of such facilities, especially EPA-mandated track pans and skimming plants. Accordingly, in 1978 E8A 400 was experimentally converted to a "fuel tender" having its emptied carbody filled with six 1350- gallon fuel tanks (former SDP40F water tanks) for a total capacity of 8100 gallons, enough for a Chicago-Seattle trip without refueling. The fuel tender requires that locomotives be fitted with trainlined fuel lines, possibly a tricky thing to do safely (though mechanically it is easy; many Western roads trainlined boiler water in the same fashion due to the limited water capacity of F3A/F7A/F9A power when equipped with dynamic braking). At press time, 400 had not been duplicated.

Ken Douglas collection, George Cockle.

PUSH-PULL POWER CARS/CAB CONTROL CARS

Push-pull commuter trains had been in use in Europe for many years when the concept was introduced in the U.S. by the Chicago & North Western in 1959. In that year, C&NW took delivery of a group of bilevel suburban coaches equipped with crew control cabs for pushing movements, thereby eliminating the need for locomotives to be turned at the outlying terminal. The principle spread to other Chicago railroads that operated suburban service and eventually was introduced to the New York City area when Central of New Jersey added control cabs to existing old cars. Long Island Rail Road and its operating agency, the Metropolitan Transportation Authority, came up with a different idea in 1970. LIRR acquired retired FA2 and FA1 carbodies from various roads and converted them to control cabs which also housed a head-end electric heating/lighting plant. In fact, it was discovered that by derating the 244 engine to 600 h.p. and applying a different generator, the means of supplying the electricity was already there. Power cars 600-618, converted in 1970-74, were joined in 1979 by 619 and 620, ex-MILW F9A and F7A. LIRR's operation has always been closely watched by the GO Transit operation in Toronto, and in 1973-74 GO converted five ex-Ontario Northland FP7's to similar power/cab-control cars. However, a GM model 149 engine was used instead of a derated prime mover to drive the alternator (900 h.p.). So, LIRR and GO avoided buying another batch of such specialized and expensive power as the GP40P or GP40TC. The GO units are numbered 9858-9862; 9858 is illustrated on following page.

Marre-Mott collection, W. J. Brennan.

John C. Allen.

GO power/cab-control car 9858 converted from an ON FP7 leads a train being pushed by GP40-2 No. 9809. By converting FP7's to power/cab-control cars, GO avoided having to buy additional GP40TC's and instead purchased less-expensive GP40-2's for motive power.

RADIO CONTROL CARS

When Radiation, Inc.'s Locotrol became the accepted means of conducting RCE (Remote Control Equipment) operation, two methods of applying the equipment became common. The first was to construct a radio control car to control the trailing consist, and the second was to apply the remote equipment directly to the locomotive (often in a specially lengthened short hood). The radio control car concept has the advantage of allowing any locomotives to be remotes, not just specially equipped units. On the other hand, most roads soon decided that they wanted only certain classes of locomotives to be remotes anyway because successful operation depends on predictable response from the remotes—something a mixed bag of engines cannot always provide. In that light, the remote-control cars were just another piece of equipment to be maintained, and they have begun to fade from the scene.

Radio control cars are ideally suited for conversion from old carbody locomotives because the necessary M.U. cables and control equipment are already at hand. The interior of such cars is mostly empty because the equipment takes up very little space. C&NW X262401 is typical of the breed: a stripped F3B with only one of its two small firecracker radio antennas visible on the roof to indicate its function. Typically, an insulated compartment within the carbody houses the equipment. Roads having such cars have included BN, L&N, C&O, and AT&SF (whose fleet of 26, Nos. 10-35, is one of the largest), and in Canada (where they are called robot cars) CPR and British Columbia Railway. The largest fleet of radio control cars is Southern's, which were purpose-built instead of converted from B units.

Marre-Mott collection, Jack Armstrong.

SLUGS AND MATES

The use of a weighted rail vehicle having traction motors but no power source of its own together with a regular locomotive goes far back into locomotive history. Starting in 1914, Butte, Anaconda & Pacific used three 40-ton "tractor trucks" M.U.'d and bussed to its electric locomotives. Back in the 1940's old Alco-GE-Ingersoll Rand box-cabs were being cut down to slugs and M.U.'d to diesel switchers for hump service. However, only with the arrival of the recent high-horsepower diesels has the idea of "road slugs" become practical (GE calls its built-to-order version a MATE for "Motors to Assist Tractive Effort"). A 2500 h.p. locomotive has power in excess of what it can use for tractive effort (for adhesion reasons) in the lower speed ranges, so it is sometimes worthwhile to haul around the weight of a slug if the dispatching of an extra unit can be avoided. The slug is only useful when starting, or in the 12 mph-or-less range where the prime-mover locomotive faces adhesion limitations.

Slugs should not be confused with brake trailers (sometimes called "sleds"), which are similar in appearance. When switching, air is usually not used on the freight cars, which means that all braking must be done with the locomotive. In kicking cars where quick decelerations are desired, this can quickly lead to flat wheels. A ballasted brake trailer provides extra wheels tied into the independent braking system of the switching locomotive and thereby spreads the braking effort and reduces flat spots. Only a few roads have used brake trailers; the common alternative is to use two M.U.'ed locomotives or in heavy switching assignments, a six-motor locomotive because of the extra horsepower.

YARD SLUGS

Canadian Pacific B100, a 1951 purpose-built unit, illustrates several features of slug design. In most respects, a slug must have the same characteristics as a locomotive underframe and running gear—independent brakes, safety appliances (handrails, steps, cut levers, etc.)—and it also must have an enclosure above the frame to house traction motor blowers. Because the slug is intended to be used in situations requiring low-speed and maximum tractive effort, motor cooling is a critical item. The enclosure on B100 shows the air inlets for the traction motor blowers. B100 is also equipped with sand fills, since a slug must be able to sand simultaneously with the prime-mover unit.

Continued

Marre-Mott collection, Larry Russell.

Also, if the slug is to be used in any way other than permanently coupled between two units, it must have a headlight. (B100's headlight is apparently salvaged from a steam locomotive.) M.U. connections are provided at both ends on B100; some slugs have the connections at one end only. CP has four slugs, B100-B103. C&NW slug BU9 illustrates how all these requirements were met by simply using an old switcher (in this case an Alco S3), de-engined. C&NW operates one of the most extensive slug fleets in yard service, slugs BU1 to BU9, converted from switchers in 1956 and 1965.

Louis A. Marre.

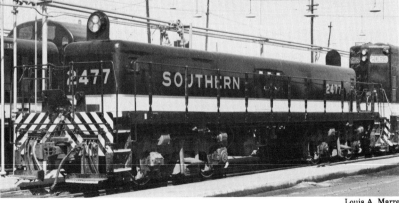

Length is no indication of whether a slug is intended for road or yard service. L&N 2059, with a prime mover from DL701 913, is used solely for yard service, but owes its length to originating in a cut-down RS3. Southern 2477 is a yard slug that is unusual in that it was scratchbuilt.

In addition to the usual M.U. connection required for connecting slugs to prime movers, bus cables are necessary for the traction current, usually a lead and a return cable for each truck if the slug operates in constant series/parallel, or has the ability to make transition. Thus, the Santa Fe example illustrated is a six-motor slug, but needs just four traction current cables. The L&N example illustrated from the side shows that the usual 27-point M.U. cable and air hoses are present, as well as the four traction-motor current cables. Because of the need for these motor connections, parent prime movers for slugs must be specially equipped.

Both photos, Louis A. Marre.

153

Marre-Mott collection, Louis A. Marre (below left), J. David Ingles (above).

In the rear view of the uncoupled RF&P slug illustrated, note that there are four traction current leads to the right and two smaller leads to the left. This is a connection for the battery charging circuit, used on many slugs (including the GE MATEs) to run the traction-motor blowers. SOU 2450/2478/2249 illustrate the concept of M.U. through a slug to a second yard unit, in this case a TR2B calf. Current for the slug must come from just one of the two units.

Santa Fe "drone" (AT&SF terminology for slugs) No. 3951 and Conrail slug 1102, both cut down from DL600's, illustrate the six-motor yard slug. For maximum effectiveness, six-motor slugs must be M.U.'ed to a prime mover larger than those usually required for four-motor slugs; 3951 is coupled to 2050 h.p. repowered DL600 No. 3900, and 1102 to SD40-2 6944. Slugs of this size are mainly useful in hump operations, which is also the most frequent employment of four-motor slugs on many roads.

Louis A. Marre.

Louis A. Marre.

ROAD SLUGS

Chicago & North Western pioneered road slugs, starting with BU10-BU12 in 1970. BU10 and BU11 were cut-down Chicago Great Western RS2's; BU12 was a converted F3B. All of C&NW's road slugs were designed to operate between pairs of GP35's, taking power from only the unit being used as the control cab. C&NW was afflicted with considerable mileage where track speed was below 30 mph; under such conditions, the road slug is an attractive concept. C&NW road slug sets BU30-BU39 were converted F3B's built in 1971. BU36 (illustrated) is one of this group. Another road slug is Columbia & Cowlitz 701B, used with Century 415 No. 701. Low speed goes with logging roads, hence the applicability of the slug concept, in this case using AAR type A trucks which are usually limited to a maximum of 45 mph.

Kenneth M. Ardinger collection, J. Wozniczka.

Marre-Mott collection, Kenneth M. Ardinger.

OC&E slugs, such as 7606, were built from ex-UP U25B's for use with EMD-repowered U25B's 7601-7605.

Kenneth M. Ardinger.

MATES

General Electric, which built the MATEs from scratch to the same under-frame dimensions as a standard U36B/U33B/U30B (the MATEs are paired with U36B's), claims two distinctions between them and road slugs: First, MATEs operate throughout a broader speed range than typical slugs (up to 30 mph on single-ended MATEs, and over the entire speed range for double-ended MATEs) and second, they are also fuel tenders, preceding Amtrak fuel tender No. 400 by seven years. The original service for which the MATEs were designed was Seaboard Coast Line's Florida phosphate service, where pairs of RS3's were handling 10,000-ton trains at low speeds. The RS3's were replaced by single U36C's with one-ended MATEs 3200-3209, delivered in 1971. In 1972, 15 double-ended MATEs, 3210-3224, were delivered to SCL for use in general road service where two six-motor units would otherwise have been assigned. The theory was that the U36B's could take a MATE with them if operating in territory where extra axles were required. The concept produced no repetitions on SCL or elsewhere.

Marre-Mott collection, J. L. Oates.

Marre-Mott collection, Don Dover.

A double-end MATE differs only in having cable and fuel hose connections at both ends. Like a slug, however, it only takes traction power from one unit at a time.

INDEX